POWER BACCARAT 2

BEAT THE CASINO PLAYING BACCARAT

Byron F. Hebert

First Edition

Hebert & Associates

ISBN 0-9635999-4-1

Library of Congress Catalog
Card Number: 98-94140

This book is dedicated to my wife Cindy and to my children Elayne, Erik, and Laura who are always a constant source of pride and inspiration.

Many thanks to James R. Katona for his constant support and assistance; no one could have a better life-long friend.

Finally, thanks to my parents Dr. Clifford and Audrey Hebert who taught me that hard work plus smart work equals success - in any endeavor.

About The Author

Byron F. Hebert has been a successful Baccarat player for many years. As a consultant, author and sports and gaming enthusiast, his gaming perspective is unique and refreshing. He writes a regular Baccarat column in *Gaming Today*, a respected weekly Las Vegas gaming publication.

POWER BACCARAT 2 is his second book on Baccarat.

TABLE OF CONTENTS

Preface

SECTION I - THE GAME OF BACCARAT

SECTION II - GAME OF OPPORTUNITIES

SECTION III - TACTICS & STRATEGIES

SECTION IV - PREPARE & PRACTICE

SECTION V - ODDS & ENDS

Preface

When common sense prevails, sound decisions are made without sophistication or special knowledge. We just know if it's too good to be true, it probably is (and often it is a rip-off).

Casino games do not favor the player. The rules and payoffs are specifically designed to give the Casino an advantage. Some games provide a greater advantage than others, and within a game, some bets more than other bets. However, this advantage is based on the long-run. In the short-run, the advantage could actually favor the player-side.

The general Casino patrons' perception varies widely; I put them into three groups. The *dreamer* is one who believes he can always fight the Casino advantage and win. The *sucker* is irresistibly attracted to the advertised get-rich-quick method. Both the *dreamer* and the *sucker* have convinced themselves that their luck or their system will make them winners. They have ignored the facts, and rationalized that they can beat the game regardless of the contrary evidence.

"One of the criteria of emotional maturity is having the ability to deal constructively with reality."
William C. Menninger

By contrast, the *Player* is one who deals with, or manages to take advantage of a given situation (Webster's definition is quite good).

A *Player* uses a strategy of short-duration play sequences, and looks for and gains from, short-term situations that lesson the Casino advantage, or even favors the player. The *Player* determines which games, and bets within these games, have the lowest Casino advantage, learns them well, and plays only those games. *Players* play Baccarat! **POWER BACCARAT 2** will show you how.

SECTION I

THE GAME OF BACCARAT

1 - Why Play Baccarat?

W hat are the best games to play, is a question frequently asked. My response first begins with a question: "*Are you really asking what games provide the best opportunity to win?*" If so, there are really only two games to play; first Baccarat, and second Craps. This answer surprises everyone because I did not include Blackjack.

I continue to be surprised by the number of people still playing Blackjack, and by comparison, how few play Baccarat. Supply and demand rule, even in a Casino. Of course I am partial to Baccarat, not because I wrote two books on the game, but because I learned from experience that the game is much easier to beat. John Scarne recommended Baccarat above all other Casino games.

How many times can you remember winning seven or more consecutive hands in Blackjack? I have won 19 hands in a row playing Baccarat, and seven straight wins is a very common occurrence.

In Blackjack, when the Dealers up-card is 9, 10, Jack, Queen, King or Ace (which occurs quite often), it is more than likely you will lose more than 60% of the time.

Additionally, the rules for Blackjack differ from Casino to Casino; one may not always have the benefit of those rules that favor the player: Surrender in particular, Doubling-down and Splitting. Consider also the small spread between the minimum and maximum bets, and the generally poor deck penetration in most Casinos dealing one or two decks. Essentially, the chips are stacked against you from the start.

Why does anyone play Blackjack? I have asked many Blackjack players this question, and their responses generally boil down to this answer: "*I know how to play, and I can enjoy myself for long periods without getting hurt.*" What they are really saying is: "*I don't know how to play the other more difficult games* (usually they are referring to Craps), *and I didn't really come here to win, I came here to have fun.*" It is therefore no great surprise why Casino's have so many Blackjack tables.

What interests me about the answers players give to this question, is that they really think they know how to play Blackjack. This is a singular view; in fact, few play the game very well. And for the few who do, they find themselves subjected to many unpleasant Casino counter-measures.

It is widely held that the average Blackjack player is giving the Casino a big advantage. The Casino advantage in Baccarat is very small, and there will be many times that the player actually has the advantage.

Consider the fact that everyone at the Black-jack table is for himself or herself, there is no camaraderie among the Players. More often than not, players are complaining about other players who acted incorrectly on their cards; "*did you see that guy, he didn't hit a 12 against the Dealers 10!*" At the Baccarat table, there are many times that everyone is betting the same way (all on PLAYER or BANK). We all win together; there is no player-requested draw of the cards (the draw of the cards is fixed by the rules).

Everyone plays to win; having fun is a side issue. Anyone who says otherwise is, at best just kidding themselves, or at worst, simply a loser. I do not know anyone who has fun losing money.

Baccarat is a game of streaks and patterns; more than any other Casino game. They offer the best wagering opportunities, and more importantly, they occur frequently. There will be many in every game. It is during these opportunities that the skillful player has a real advantage over the Casino. There is no other Casino game that this occurs so often.

You can wager as little as $5, or as much as $5,000 per hand (often much more). During these streak and pattern opportunities some very serious cash can be won (or lost). That is why Baccarat is the game of choice for the high-rollers, few play Blackjack.

Finally, why is Baccarat better to play than Craps? There are two main reasons: first, there are many more favorable opportunities, and second, Baccarat is a whole lot simpler to play.

It is not that Craps is overly complicated, it is just that most people think it is, and therefore, do not try to learn. Baccarat is also widely viewed as being a complicated game; this of course is a myth. In fact, Baccarat is the easiest Casino game to play.

Both games are fun, but Craps has the edge when there is a good roll going. However, the good rolls are few and far between, and those monster rolls you hear about are very rare.

Baccarat, on the other hand, provides many good opportunities in every Shoe. The common streaks and patterns often give the skillful player an advantage over the Casino. These streaks and patterns come in all forms and kinds. For example, consecutive win streaks by BANK or PLAYER perhaps are the best opportunities. Winning streaks of 5 to 9 straight are fairly common, and I have seen as many as 23 straight by BANK.

Tie pattern opportunities are also very profitable; win one, and they pay 8 to 1. I consistently win the majority of my TIE bets based on pattern tie wagering. I have won as many as 13 out of 15 total TIE's in a Shoe.

The Casino advantage is also less than Craps, and the skill needed to become a winning Baccarat player is less difficult to achieve than the same level of skill necessary to be successful at Craps.

Another major advantage for Baccarat is that one can play with a much smaller bankroll; as little as $5 per hand. To correctly play Craps, one would typically have three or more bets, plus odds (on PASS and COME), working at the same time on each toss of the dice.

This can get very expensive after a few early 7-outs.

Baccarat is also a first-class game. In the pit the Dealers wear tuxedoes, and free sandwiches are sometimes served. There are no players bumping into you, or looking over your shoulder. Under such circumstances it much easier to concentrate.

Ironically, the nature of the pit seems to be one of the major reasons more people do not play Baccarat. The pit looks too intimidating! If so, play Mini-Baccarat. These tables are located on the general Casino floor, and look like a Blackjack table. Players are always sitting down to play Blackjack not realizing the table is actually a Mini-Baccarat table.

> *"A determined soul will do more with a rusty monkey wrench, than a loafer will accomplish with all the tools in a machine shop."*
> *Rupert Hughes*

The bottom line: Baccarat is easy to play, fun, and most importantly, it is the only Casino game that can be consistently beat with the proper skill and discipline. For my money, Baccarat is THE game!

2 - How The Game Is Played

The word Baccarat is pronounced bak-a'-ra, the "t" is silent. It is played with eight decks of regular playing cards that are dealt out of a Shoe, either by the players themselves at the big Baccarat table in the pit, or by the Dealer at the Mini-Baccarat table.

Only two hands are dealt, one for the PLAYER and one for the BANK. Prior to the start (deal) of any hand, each player makes his/her wager on either the BANK or the PLAYER. The values of the cards in each of the two hands are totaled, according to the prescribed rules, and the closest hand to a total of 9 wins. In Baccarat, you are always in the game. You can never break or bust as in Blackjack.

You can also wager that the two hands will be the same or "tie". TIE bets can be made along with a wager on the BANK or PLAYER. Winning TIE bets pay 8 to 1. If there is a tie, all BANK and PLAYER bets are not affected, and you may remove your bets, or change them as you wish. Winning PLAYER wagers pay even money. Winning BANK hand bets pay 95 cents on the dollar; a 5% commission is charged on all winning BANK bets because the rules slightly favor the BANK. Some Casino's charge only a 4% commission.

To keep the game moving, winning BANK wagers
are paid even money, and the 5% commissions
are tallied and accumulated by the Dealer using small colored markers. At the conclusion
of the Shoe, all commissions must be paid.
Commissions, in whole or in part, can also be
paid at any time during the game.

Over the long run, and including TIE's, the
BANK hand wins 1.23 percent more often than
the PLAYER hand wins. Baccarat has the lowest
Casino advantage of any game in the Casino.

3 - Card Values And Totals

PLAYER or BANK hands may consist of 2 or 3 cards, no more. The number of cards given (2 or 3) is determined by the prescribed rules of play.

The value of the cards from Ace through 9 have the same value as their spot or pip count. Thus, the Ace is 1, the deuce is 2, and so on to 9, which has a value of 9.

The 10's, Jacks, Queens, and Kings have no value; they are 0. The suits of Spades, Clubs, Hearts, and Diamonds have no meaning or value either.

The cards dealt to each hand are simply totaled. However, no hand can exceed 9. Thus, the first digit of any total over 9 is dropped. A hand of 8 and 6 totals 14, dropping the first digit makes the total 4.

A hand of Jack/Queen is zero. Any total of zero is called Baccarat, the lowest hand in the game.

A hand of 3 and 6 is 9. The best hand in Baccarat is any total of 9. Two card totals of 8 or 9 are called *naturals*.

The calculation of the card-totals is quite simple. The series of hands listed in Table 1 should clear up any confusion.

Example Baccarat Hands

Cards	Total
10 - KING	0
KING - JACK	0
7 - 6	3
8 - 2	0
ACE - 9	0
6 - 5	1
4 - 8 - 6	8
KING - QUEEN - 10	0
4 - JACK - ACE	5
7 - 7	4
8 - 4 - 9	1

Table 1

4 - Rules of Play

The rules for Baccarat are the same in all American Casinos. The Casino will provide a printed card of the rules on request. Figure 1 is an example of a rules card. Typically, the rules are printed on the reverse side of the scorecards provided by the Casino.

The object of the game is to win the hand you have wagered on by having a higher total than the other hand. The closer the total is to 9, the best hand in Baccarat, the better your chances of winning. Remember, only two hands are dealt, one for the BANK and one for the PLAYER.

All players make their wagers before the start of any deal. An initial draw of two cards for the PLAYER and two cards for the BANK is completed. A total of 8 or 9 on the initial two-card draw is called a natural; an automatic winner against any lower total, and no more cards are drawn for either hand. The hand is over.

If both hands have a natural, the higher one wins. If there is a tie then neither hand wins or loses, and a new hand is dealt. If, after the first two cards, there are no naturals for either the PLAYER or BANK, then the other rules of play are followed.

The PLAYER hand always acts first, and only after that, does the BANK hand act, either standing or drawing another card.

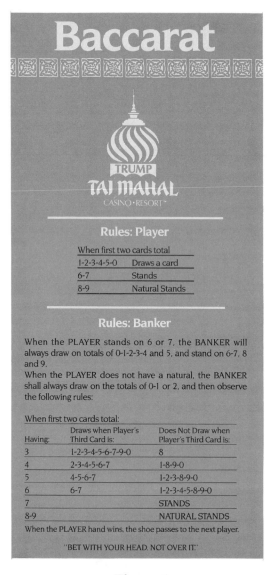

Baccarat

TRUMP
TAJ MAHAL
CASINO · RESORT™

Rules: Player

When first two cards total	
1-2-3-4-5-0	Draws a card
6-7	Stands
8-9	Natural Stands

Rules: Banker

When the PLAYER stands on 6 or 7, the BANKER will always draw on totals of 0-1-2-3-4 and 5, and stand on 6-7, 8 and 9.

When the PLAYER does not have a natural, the BANKER shall always draw on the totals of 0-1 or 2, and then observe the following rules:

When first two cards total:

Having:	Draws when Player's Third Card is:	Does Not Draw when Player's Third Card is:
3	1-2-3-4-5-6-7-9-0	8
4	2-3-4-5-6-7	1-8-9-0
5	4-5-6-7	1-2-3-8-9-0
6	6-7	1-2-3-4-5-8-9-0
7		STANDS
8-9		NATURAL STANDS

When the PLAYER hand wins, the shoe passes to the next player.

"BET WITH YOUR HEAD, NOT OVER IT."

Figure 1

The PLAYER hand rules are very simple and are summarized as follows:

1: Totals of 8 or 9: naturals; no third card is drawn for either PLAYER or BANK. The hand is over.

2: Totals of 6 or 7: PLAYER stands; does not draw a third card.

3: Totals of 0-1-2-3-4-5: PLAYER draws a third card (of course only if BANK does not have a natural 8 or 9).

The BANK hand rules are a little more complicated. The BANK draws a third card (or not) based on its total, and if applicable, the face value of the third card that was drawn by the PLAYER hand. The BANK hand rules are summarized as follows for each of the listed two-card totals:

1: Totals of 8 or 9: naturals; no third card is drawn for either BANK or PLAYER. The hand is over.

2: Total of 7: BANK stands; does not draw a third card.

3: Total of 6: BANK stands **IF** PLAYER did not draw a third card.

But, if PLAYER drew a third card, BANK only draws when PLAYERS third card was a 6 or 7. BANK does not draw a third card when PLAYERS third card was 0-1-2-3-4-5-8-9.

4: Total of 5: BANK draws a third card **IF** PLAYERS third card was 4-5-6-7. BANK does not draw a third card when PLAYERS third card was 0-1-2-3-8-9.

5:    Total of 4: BANK draws a third card **IF**
      PLAYERS third card was a 2-3-4-5-6-7.
      BANK does not draw a third card when
      PLAYERS third card was 0-1-8-9.

6:    Total of 3: BANK draws a third card **IF**
      PLAYERS third card was 0-1-2-3-4-5-6-7-
      9. BANK does not draw a third card when
      PLAYERS third card was an 8.

7:    Totals of 0-1-2: BANK always draws a
      third card.

Lets review the BANK rules once again since
they are more complex. First, what does the
BANK do if the PLAYER <u>does not</u> draw a third
card, and PLAYER does <u>not</u> have a natural (the
PLAYER must then have 6 or 7)?

In this case, the rules for the BANK are the
same as they are for the PLAYER, which are:
1.   The BANK always draws to totals of 0-1-
      2-3-4-5 and stands on totals of 6-7-8-9.

Alternatively, if PLAYER <u>does</u> draw a third
card, that is, the PLAYER had an initial two-
card total of 0-1-2-3-4-5 (the BANK would obviously not have an 8 or 9 because there
would be no draw for either hand), the easiest way to remember the rules are:
2.   BANK has 0-1-2: BANK always draws no
      matter what PLAYERS third card was.

3.   BANK has 3: BANK draws every time <u>except</u>
      when PLAYERS third card was 8.

4.   BANK has 6: BANK stands <u>except</u> when
      PLAYER draws a 6 or 7.

5.   BANK has 7: BANK always stands.

The rules not covered above are when the BANK has a total of 4 or 5; the hardest rules to memorize.

6. When BANK has 4: BANK <u>stands</u> when PLAYERS third card is either the two lowest cards of 0-1, or the two highest cards of 8 or 9. BANK <u>draws</u> a third card on any other third card value given to the PLAYER (2-3-4-5-6-7).

7. When BANK has 5: BANK <u>draws</u> a third card when PLAYERS third card is the middle card values of 4-5-6-7. BANK <u>stands</u> on all the other card values (0-1-2-3-8-9).

These are the automatic rules of the card-draw. Memorize them because Dealers occasionally make mistakes, nearly always at the Mini-Baccarat tables. Rarely are mistakes made at the big Baccarat tables since there is more than one Dealer, and the table is watched more closely by supervision.

In addition to occasional mistakes made at the Mini-Baccarat tables, you may find a Dealer who will cheat for tokes or tips.

A Dealer could purposely deal, or not deal, a third card, contrary to the rules, to assist a player who has been tipping. For example, the tipper has a big bet on the BANK, and also a bet on the BANK for the Dealer. You have a bet on PLAYER. The first two cards are dealt and PLAYER has 5, BANK has 4. The rules call for the PLAYER to draw a third card; an Ace is drawn giving the PLAYER hand a total of 6.

The rules state that the BANK does <u>not</u> draw. Instead, the Dealer knowing that BANK loses, draws a third card for the BANK anyway hoping for a win; a 3 is drawn and Dealer announces the BANK win since this would give BANK a total of 7. Of course the real winner should be PLAYER, 6 to 4.

Unless you know the rules, you could not prevent a Dealer from cheating you. Even if you did catch the Dealer cheating, the Dealer would merely claim it was a mistake. The Casino Supervisor would support your objection, and you would be paid for your PLAYER win.

"It is discouraging how many people are shocked by honesty and how few by deceit."

Noel Coward

Therefore:
1. Learn the rules to protect your interest.
2. Speak-up if an error occurs; do not allow the hand to be discarded until you get a ruling from the Casino Supervisor.

5 - The 5% Commission Thing

All winning BANK wagers are charged a 5% commission. A winning $100 bet on the BANK will cost $5 ($4 in the Casino's charging a 4% commission). The Dealer will pay the player $100, and place a $5 dollar marker in the numbered box, located in front of the chip tray, that corresponds to the players seat number. These buttons will be used by the Dealer to maintain a running total of the commission owed to the Casino by each player. No commission is charged on winning PLAYER wagers.

At the conclusion of the 8-deck Shoe, the Dealer will collect the total commission amounts due from each player. However, it is recommended that commissions owed be paid-off or reduced as the game progresses. At any time during the game you may pay all, or any part of the commission due. But, do this only occasionally; constant commission payments slow-down the game and can break your concentration. Frequent interruptions of play to pay commissions are also very annoying to the other players, and a nuisance to the Dealer.

The best time to pay-off or reduce a commission is when you are getting change for higher denomination chips. It is also best to reduce commissions when they have accumulated to a fairly high dollar amount.

It will be easier to keep track of the commissions you owe when they are for smaller
dollar amounts.

Yes, you must carefully watch the Dealers
calculate and post the commissions, they
sometimes make mistakes. Dealers first have
to calculate the amount of the commission
based on the actual winning BANK wager, and
then add it to the existing total already
posted. When winning numerous BANK wagers,
frequent changes will be made to your commission total using different denomination buttons. As a result, mathematical errors can be
made, and unless you pay attention, you could
be in for a surprise at the end of the Shoe.

Dealers have also been known to post a commission to the wrong player, or mistakenly
charge a commission for a PLAYER win. In any
case, you want to be able to point-out the
mistake when it occurs, not later when it
will be very difficult getting the Casino to
see it your way.

6 - The Real Casino Advantage

The typical misinformed player reasons "*Why play Baccarat and pay 5% when I can play Craps or Blackjack and pay no commission?*" I have already covered all the reasons to play Baccarat instead of Blackjack and Craps, and stated that Baccarat has the lowest Casino advantage. Lets examine the Casino advantage for Baccarat more closely. Of course one way of comparing games is to look at the Casino advantage of each game.

The Casino advantage for Craps is 1.41% on the PASS LINE, and 1.40% on the DON'T PASS LINE. For Blackjack, the Casino advantage varies according to the rules allowed by the individual Casino, and the ability or skill of the player. I believe an average Blackjack player typically faces a Casino advantage of at least 5%, and without favorable rules, the advantage to the Casino is much greater.

What then is the Casino advantage for Baccarat? Over the long-run and including TIE's, BANK wins 45.84% of the time, PLAYER wins 44.61% of the time. TIE's, when neither the BANK nor PLAYER wins or losses, occur 9.55% of the time. The automatic rules of the game are such that BANK wins more often; exactly 1.23% more often. This is the reason you will be charged a 5% commission on all winning BANK wagers.

But, the 5% commission is **NOT** the Casino advantage. The Casino advantage for BANK is in fact a paltry 1.06%. It is calculated as follows: 44.61% of the time a $100 bet on BANK will lose $44.61, and 45.84% of the time a $100 bet on BANK will win $43.55 (this is because you win only $95 due to the 5% commission being applied to the $100 bet). The difference between 44.61 and 43.55 is 1.06%, far less than 5%, and even less than the Casino advantage for Craps and Blackjack.

The Casino advantage is slightly different for PLAYER, and is calculated in the same manner, but there is no commission applied to winning PLAYER bets. Thus for PLAYER, the advantage is simply the difference between 45.84 and 44.61, or 1.23%; still a very low advantage.

7 - Scoring

Baccarat is a game of frequent streaks and patterns in the outcomes of the decisions. These streaks and patterns provide the best wagering opportunities. To gain the most profit from these opportunities, the player has to recognize them, and do so as quickly as possible. First, one must have at least a good knowledge base of the various kinds of streaks and patterns so typical in the game of the Baccarat (which will be covered in detail later). Second, a good player will use an organized method of recording the decisions of the outcomes as the game progresses.

Keeping a scorecard of the decisions and applying a consistent scoring technique is absolutely essential. The Casino will provide a blank scorecard and pencil/pen upon request. In the heat of the action and at a glance, you will be able to spot those frequent streaks and patterns that make Baccarat the most profitable player-game in the Casino.

The Casino will usually have two or three types of scorecards to choose from. I prefer to use a shorter scorecard that can be used to record the decision outcomes vertically, rather than horizontally. I also prefer a pencil instead of a pen.

Figure 2 shows an example of one of my completed scorecards. The scoring technique I
use is fairly simple. First, keep a separate
running total of the hands won by both the
BANK and the PLAYER sides. The scorecard
shows that BANK wins hand #1, indicated by
the #1 under the BANK column. PLAYER wins the
next nine non-TIE decisions, recorded separately on the scorecard for each decision,
number 1 through 9 under the PLAYER column.
BANK won the next non-TIE decision, its second win, as indicated by the #2 under the
BANK column. Continue in this manner decision
by decision. At any time during play, you
will know exactly which side is more dominant. In the example, after 11 non-TIE decisions, PLAYER has won 9 hands to 2 for BANK.

Second, as you record a separate running total of the decisions won by PLAYER and BANK,
circle those numbered outcomes that are won,
as indicated by the circled decision numbers
on the scorecard. I won seven out of the
first 11 non-TIE decisions.

Third, write "T" or "TIE" for any TIE decisions, and circle them when you win a TIE
bet. I record them as TIE-1, TIE-2, and so on
to keep track of the number of TIE decisions
as the Shoe is played-out.

Fourth, when you decide not to make a bet on
a given hand(s), cross out the number(s) corresponding to the running totals being recorded for each decision. Remember, unlike
Blackjack where you must play every hand, in
Baccarat you can sit-out or skip hands. Simply don't bet and tell the Dealer *No bet*.
This is accepted as a normal part of the
game.

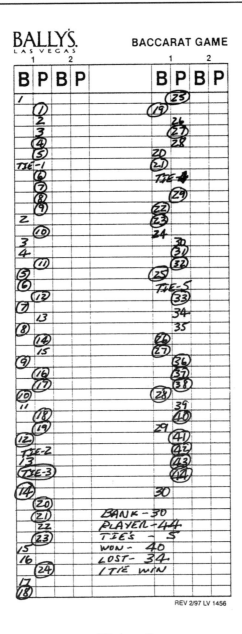

Figure 2

Keep recording the outcomes as you move down the paired BANK and PLAYER columns. Record each individual decision in the appropriate BANK or PLAYER column. In this manner, the streaks, patterns and trends in the outcomes will be clearly visible. Keep the scorecard neat and tidy, they are much easier to read.

Before you sit down to play an in-progress game, determine the current trend; has PLAYER won 7 consecutive decisions, or is the pattern of outcomes alternating back and forth between PLAYER and BANK. Ask the players, the Dealers, or look at the scorecards kept by the players. If you do decide to play, stick with the current trend. If PLAYER is on a winning streak, bet PLAYER.

You can keep score or chart the game before you play. Simply stand behind the table and keep score of the outcomes. When it appears that a favorable opportunity is presented, begin to play. Some Casino's have installed electronic scoreboards; you can use them to monitor a game for favorable opportunities before deciding to play. But, once you decide to play keep your own scorecard. I prefer to play full-Shoes, not partial Shoes, unless there is a good opportunity.

I also suggest that notes and statistics be recorded; date, time, number of Shoes played, starting buy-in or bankroll at the beginning of the Shoe, and profit/loss statistics after the Shoe is completed.

After each Shoe I critically review my scorecard paying particular attention to any difficult sequences. This helps me focus on eliminating mistakes.

Summarize the results; number of hands won by PLAYER and BANK, number of TIE's, total number of hands, number of hands won (number of circled numbers), number of TIE's won (number of circled TIE's) and number of hands not bet.

> "Like Business, Baccarat is a combination of war and sport."
>
> Byron F. Hebert

After each trip, I add my scorecards to my statistical database. Over the years this critical evaluation process has significantly improved my technique, helped me establish a consistent and disciplined approach to play, and most importantly, helped me win and win often! It can work for you just as well. Keeping score is an essential part of the process.

8 - The Big Table

The big Baccarat tables are usually located in a separate room or roped-off area of the Casino known as the pit. The table itself has fourteen seats for players. On the table in front of each chair is a large numeral to identify the player. These numerals range from #1 to #15 (there is no seat #13). Seven players can be accommodated on each end of the table.

Three Dealers direct the game from the center of the table. Two Dealers sit on one side and are responsible for collections, payoffs, and keeping track of the commissions owed to the Casino by each player.

In front of the Dealers is the chip box, and in front of that are small boxes, numbered 1 through 15 (with the #13 missing). Coins and buttons cover the appropriate boxes, corresponding to the commission owed by each player by seat number. For example, if the player in seat 8 owes $10 in commissions, this amount is shown in the small box numbered 8 in front of the Dealer.

Commissions are not due or payable after every hand. They are due at the end of the Shoe, when the cards have all been dealt, or when the player decides to leave the game. The player may also pay their commission at any time during the game.

Also in the center, directly across from the two sitting Dealers, stands the Caller. The Caller directs the game, and is responsible for making sure that the proper number of cards are dealt, and that no bets are made after the first card of the hand is removed from the Shoe. He/she also observes the two Dealers who first collect losing wagers, and then pay winning bets. Like the Stickman in Craps, the Caller encourages players to bet on the tie, the bet with highest Casino advantage. At specific times this can be a good bet, as you will see later.

There will also be one or two Supervisors present. Their function is to protect the game. They watch carefully to ensure that the cards are properly mixed and shuffled before the start of the game, and that winners are paid correctly. Any disputes that occur are directed to their attention, and he or she usually has the final word in settling any arguments between the players and the Dealers.

Disputes are rare, since there are no optional plays in Baccarat. But occasionally, a player may claim that the pay-off or commission due is incorrect. The Supervisor will make the decision or refer the dispute to the Pit Boss. In a big money game, the Pit Boss, the Shift Boss, and sometimes even the Casino Manager, will observe the game. During these occasions, maximum bets could be raised to six figures to accommodate the high rollers.

Typically the maximum bet is $5,000. However, I have played when individual players are wagering well in excess of $20,000 per hand.

Baccarat is played with eight decks of regular playing cards. When the table opens, eight fresh decks of cards are unwrapped. Each deck is spread out face-up, with all 52 cards showing to allow the Dealers and the players to examine the cards, and make sure all is in order. The eight decks are merged and two Dealers are each handed half the stack to mix. There is considerable shuffling and then the Dealer retrieves both stacks and shuffles all 416 cards together.

These cards will give an average of 80 hands, 73 hands when either the BANK or PLAYER hands win, and 7 tie's.

After the cards are shuffled, the cards are laced or salted. This ensures that the decks are not stacked. To do this, the Dealer removes a full deck or more from the front of the stack of cards and "salts" them into the remaining stack by inserting these cards a few at a time until they are all spread throughout the remaining decks.

After the shuffle and lacing, the Caller offers a blank white or yellow plastic indicator card to a player with one hand, while holding the eight decks together with the other hand. The player accepting the indicator inserts it into the deck to cut the cards.

A line of cards from the back of the deck is then spread out (face down) on the table. The Dealer counts fourteen cards from back to front and inserts another indicator. These fourteen cards, plus any extra, are returned to the back of the deck. Eighty or so hands later, when the first indicator card appears, it is the signal for the Caller to announce:

"The next hand will be the last hand of this Shoe." This card-mixing procedure does vary from Casino to Casino, but generally follows the methods previously outlined. Some Casinos use shuffle machines to shuffle the cards instead of the time-consuming manual method.

The eight decks are then placed in the Shoe and the Caller removes the first card. The face value of the card determines the number of cards to be burned or discarded. These are usually dealt face down then dropped into the discard slot on the table, where they fall into a large bucket beneath the table so they can be retrieved for reuse. A four means four cards are discarded. A picture card means that ten cards are burned.

In the Baccarat pit the players, not the Dealers, deal the cards. Each player has a chance to handle the Shoe. The two hands dealt-out by the holder of the Shoe affect all participants at the table. The cards dealt to the BANK hand affect all the players betting on BANK, even though they do not handle those cards. Whether the player sits in seat number 1 or seat number 15 makes no difference.

In front of each player is the numbered position, and in front of each number are three additional boxes, one-marked **PLAYERS** (PLAYER hand), one **BANKERS** (BANK hand), and one for **TIE**. If players wish to bet on the PLAYER hand, they place their chips in the box marked for the PLAYER bets. To bet on BANK, they place their chips in the box marked for the BANK bets. To bet on a TIE, the chips are placed in the small numbered box above the BANK bet.

Now the game is ready and the Caller announces: *"Place your bets, Baccarat is about to begin."*

The Caller slides the Shoe to the player sitting in the seat behind numeral #1, but cautions the player to wait until he/she (the Caller) asks for the cards to be dealt. The game has started. Lets review a couple typical hands to give you a flavor for this exciting game.

The Caller passes the Shoe to the player who will deal. This player will continue to deal as long as the BANK hand keeps winning, and that could be for 1 hand, or 15 or more consecutive decisions. Since a tie is not a loss, the player retains the Shoe and the deal. Incidentally, you do not have to handle the Shoe, simply pass it to the next player. The deal goes (all cards face down):

First card: center of the table (toward the Caller).

Second card: next to the Shoe.

Third card: center of the table (toward the Caller)

Fourth card: next to the Shoe.

The first and third cards belong to the PLAYER hand, and all who are betting on PLAYER. The second and fourth cards belong to the BANK hand, and all players wagering on BANK. No more cards are dealt at this point.

The Caller then passes the PLAYER hand (cards face down) to the person who has made the largest wager on PLAYER.

This person looks at the PLAYER hand and tosses it face-up in middle of table (toward the Caller). Often players will look at the cards rather slowly at which time the Caller will again request the cards.

The Caller announces the total of the PLAYER hand, for example an 8, and says: *"There will be no draw, PLAYER has a natural 8."*

The player dealing and holding the Shoe, takes the BANK hand and tosses it face up in center of table. Again this player could take some time to do this.

The Caller announces the total of the BANK hand, for example a 9, another natural and Caller says: *"BANK has a natural 9, BANK wins 9 over 8."* The Dealers will collect all losing PLAYER bets, and pay even money on BANK bets. The Dealers then put the applicable 5% commission markers in the appropriate spots for those players that bet on the winning BANK hand. All players again make their bets as the same person dealing prepares to deal a new hand. Play keeps going on, hand after hand around the table, with a new player taking over the Shoe and the deal whenever the PLAYER hand wins. Once the cards are given to the Caller each hand is concluded in a matter of seconds.

The BANK won the previous hand, so the same player continues to hold the Shoe and deal the cards for the next hand.

PLAYER hand is dealt a 9 and 6; Caller announces *"PLAYER has 5."* BANK hand is dealt a 3 and 2; Caller announces *"BANK has 5, card for the Player."*

A 6 is drawn, Caller announces *"PLAYER is reduced to 1, card for the BANK."* BANK must draw a third card according to the prescribed automatic rules.

The third card for the BANK is a 5; Caller announces *"BANK is reduced to 0, PLAYER wins 1 over 0, the Shoe moves."*

What a nice draw if you had wagered on the PLAYER, and a terrible draw if you had bet on the BANK. Such is the exciting game of Baccarat.

9 - Mini-Baccarat

Baccarat is the only Casino game that is played on two different tables; one on the big table in the Baccarat Pit, and one on the little table, the smaller Mini-Baccarat table. Mini-Baccarat contains space for seven players. The big table in the Pit holds fourteen players. Both games are dealt out of an eight deck Shoe. The rules, commissions, odds and payoffs are also the same at both tables, but the betting limits at the big table are usually higher; minimums $25 to $100 and maximums $5,000 to $10,000. Mini-Baccarat limits are typically $5 to $25, and $1,000 to $3,000.

Because of their location in the Pit or in a side room off the general Casino floor, the big tables are more intimidating to less experienced players. The Pit caters to the high rollers. Mini-Baccarat is less threatening due to its location on the general Casino floor. In addition to the differences in location and surroundings, the games are also dealt differently and the speed of the action can be quite different.

In the pit, there are three Dealers. But, the players themselves handle the Shoe. That is, the players deal the cards from the Shoe. Each time the PLAYER hand wins, the Shoe moves to the next player who will deal the next hand.

Each player has an opportunity to deal the cards, and players who prefer not to deal can pass the Shoe to the next player.

The player with the highest wager on the PLAYER hand receives the PLAYER hand cards. The player holding the Shoe has the BANK hand cards. These players examine the cards before tossing them toward the standing Dealer, known as the Caller. Some ritualistic routines that players go through when looking at the cards are very time-consuming, and can become very annoying. They are annoying because I find it more difficult to get into a rhythm.

I recall one player who would take a lot of time squeezing the cards, and crush the cards into a ball when he did not like them. As a result, the action at the big table is occasionally very slow. The Casino tolerates this slower pace since at the big table hundreds of thousands of dollars can be in-action on every hand.

However, unlike play at the big table none of the players handle the Shoe or the cards at the Mini-Baccarat table. At the Mini-Baccarat table one Dealer handles the entire game. The dealer shuffles the cards (the cards are now usually shuffled by a machine, not manually by the Dealers as they are in the Pit), deals them face up, calls the game, collects losing bets, makes payoffs, and keeps track of the commissions owed on all winning BANK hand bets.

Because there is only one Dealer, disputes are more common. Mistakes are sometimes made in calling the game or posting commissions. Thus, it is important for players to know all of the third-card draw rules, and carefully watch the Dealer post commissions.

The Mini-Baccarat table is about the same size as a Blackjack table, the markings on the layout are much different; they conform to the big Baccarat table layout. Many times I have sat at the Mini-table and a Blackjack player will sit down not realizing it is a Baccarat table; what does this tell you about a Blackjack player that doesn't recognize he is sitting at the wrong table?

Each player, places his or her chips in the appropriately numbered box or circle in front of them when wagering on any of the available bets on the layout: PLAYER hand, BANK hand, or TIE.

The action at the Mini-Baccarat tables will be faster, sometimes much faster, than the action at the big tables. A Mini-Baccarat player will therefore have much less time to think about his or her wagering strategy between hands.

One other difference you may find at the Mini tables is the handling of commissions. At some Casino's when a bet is made on BANK, the corresponding commission is also put out.

That is, the commission amount is calculated by the player and placed on the table along with the bet on the BANK. In such games the table layout has a spot marked for the commission. If the BANK wins, the Dealer pays off the winning BANK bet and takes the commission or provides change if the player did not put out the exact or correct amount.

Still in other Casino's, instead of actually placing the commission on the table along with a bet on BANK, the Casino will collect the commission due after each BANK win.

Each game has its pluses and minuses. Baccarat in the Pit is slower, but minimum bets are typically higher. Mini-Baccarat has lower minimums, but it is played at a faster pace. If Mini-Baccarat suits you better, sit-out a few hands when the pace gets too fast. Either way, big or little, Baccarat is still the best Casino game.

10 - Section Review and Summary

Why You Should Play Baccarat:

1. The Casino advantage is the lowest of all Casino games.
2. It is the simplest game to play. Only two decisions are necessary: how much to bet and what to wager on.
3. There are no options or decisions for the player to make as the cards are dealt; the rules are automatic. As such, there are no complaints about player decisions to hit or stand as in Blackjack. In Baccarat you can never break or bust.
4. It is fast-paced and exciting; a lot of money can be in action.
5. There are frequent runs or streaks that offer many excellent opportunities; many more than Craps and Blackjack.
6. There is no difference in the rules from Casino to Casino as in Blackjack.
7. There is a large spread between minimum and maximum bets.
8. Players with a small bankrolls can play.
9. It is the game of choice for high-rollers.
10. It is easy to concentrate in the Baccarat pit since you will not be bumped or jostled.
11. It is a class-game; players often develop a camaraderie.
12. Baccarat is the perfect game for a systems player, and it takes less time to become an advanced player.

This is what John Scarne said about playing Baccarat in his book *Scarne's Complete Guide to Gambling*:

*"If you still insist on casino gambling after having read this book, and you find yourself in a casino that harbors all the standard casino games, and you would like to give yourself the **best possible chance to win**, sit yourself down at the Baccarat table."*

I highlighted the words *best possible chance to win* because obviously winning is your first objective!

Object of the Game:

Two hands are dealt, the BANK hand and the PLAYER hand. Prior to the deal, each player wagers on either the BANK hand or the PLAYER hand (or on the TIE, which can be made along with a bet on the BANK or PLAYER). Whichever of the two hands (BANK or PLAYER) is closest to 9 is the winner.

Casino Advantage:

The PLAYER has 44.61 percent probability of winning and 45.84 percent probability of losing. The Casino advantage on BANK bets is 1.06 percent, and on PLAYER bets 1.23 percent. This is the lowest Casino advantage among all the table games.

The only bet that offers a lower Casino edge is the Craps line bets with double or more odds. However, to get this lower Casino advantage requires the outlay of significantly more money.

Payoffs:

All winning PLAYER hand wagers are paid even money. All winning BANK hand wagers are paid 95 cents to every dollar wagered because the player must pay a 5 percent commission on the amount won. All winning TIE bets (when the BANK hand and PLAYER hand totals are equal) are paid 8 to 1. In such cases, the BANK hand and PLAYER hand wagers are not affected, and they can be changed or removed.

Card Values and Totals:

All tens and picture cards have a value of 0. The Ace counts as 1, and the remaining cards 2 through 9 are counted at face value. The four suits have no meaning or value.

The best Baccarat hand is a total of 9. If the total of the hand exceeds 9, it is adjusted simply by dropping the first digit. For example, a hand of 8, 7 and 7 is 22, which is 2. Thus the only possible totals are 0 to 9.

Rules of Play:

After the initial two-card draw to the PLAYER hand and BANK hand, the automatic draw rules determine if another card is drawn. Only one additional card can be drawn to either or both hands.

The following rules determine whether either or both hands must draw a third card:

Rule 1: If either hand totals 8 or 9 (called a natural), the hand is over; both hands must stand. If <u>neither</u> hand has a natural, PLAYER hand must act first.

Rule 2: If after the initial two-card draw, PLAYER hand totals 0-1-2-3-4-5, the PLAYER hand must draw a third card. If the initial total is 6 or 7, PLAYER hand must stand.

Rule 3: BANK always stands with an initial two-card total of 7.

Rule 4: When PLAYER hand stands on 6 and 7, then the third card rules for the BANK hand are the same as the PLAYER hand (BANK hand draws a third card to totals or 0-1-2-3-4-5 and stands on totals of 6 and 7.).

Rule 5: When PLAYER hand draws a third card, BANK hand must stand or draw as shown in Table 2. They are referred to as the automatic third-card-draw rules for BANK. The draw decisions are made according to these rules. The Dealer will always announce if a draw is required according to these rules.

Refer to the additional examples illustrating all of the rules in Table 3.

Automatic Third-Card Draw Rules For BANK

BANK Hand Two Card Total	Draws When PLAYER Third Card Is:	Stands When PLAYER Third Card Is:
0, 1, 2	Any Card	Not Applicable
3	0 to 7, and 9	8
4	2 to 7	0, 1, 8 and 9
5	4, 5, 6 and 7	0 to 3, 8 and 9
6	6 and 7	0 to 5, 8 and 9
7	Not Applicable	Any Card

Table 2

Minimum & Maximum Wagers:

Casinos offer Baccarat at $5 to $25 minimum bet, and $1,000 to $5,000 maximum bet. Minimums and maximums vary based on playing demand. Minimum bet increases during play require that notice be given to all players. All existing players will not be bound to the new higher minimum bet; they may continue to bet the old lower amount. Maximums are often increased for high-rollers.

> *"It is the studying that you do after your school days that really counts. Otherwise, you only know that which everyone else knows."*
> *Henry L. Doherty*

Guidelines & Rules for Disciplined Play:

1. Memorize the automatic draw rules to protect your interest. Speak-up if an error occurs; do not allow the hand to be discarded until you get a ruling from the Casino Supervisor.
2. Carefully watch the Dealers total and post your commissions for winning BANK wagers, they sometimes make mistakes.
3. Pay-off or reduce your commissions when obtaining change for higher denomination chips.
4. Also pay-off or reduce your commissions when they have accumulated to a fairly high dollar total; it will be easier to keep track of the commissions you owe when they are for smaller dollar amounts.
5. Keep interruptions of play to a minimum; frequent payments of commissions and changing currency for additional chips are very annoying to the other players, and a nuisance for the Dealer.
6. Keep a scorecard of each decision as the Shoe is played-out, and apply a consistent scoring technique. Keep completed scorecards for later review and analysis.
7. Before you sit down to play in a game that is in-progress, determine the current pattern or trend. Do <u>not</u> bet against the trend.

Wrap-up

If you have never played Baccarat before, your first lesson is now complete. If you have played before, perhaps you have a new or refreshed perspective. The basic guidelines and rules covered in this Section are the foundation; all else builds upon them.

What you take away from the rest of POWER
BACCARAT 2, and how you apply it, depends on
the effort you are willing to make to learn
the skills and techniques of winning play.

Additional Rules Examples

PLAYER Hand Cards	BANK Hand Cards	Rule Explanation
2 and 1	4 and 4	Both hands stand (Rule 1)
4 and 2	2 and KING	PLAYER hand stands (Rule 2) BANK hand draws (Rule 4)
6 and QUEEN	ACE and 6	PLAYER hand stands (Rule 2) BANK hand stands (Rule 3)
4 and 3	JACK and 6	PLAYER hand stands (Rule 2) BANK hand stands (Rule 4)
ACE and 6	QUEEN and 10	PLAYER hand stands (Rule 2) BANK hand draws (Rule 4)
4 and 1	10 and 7	PLAYER hand draws (Rule 2) BANK hand stands (Rule 3)
ACE and 10	and 3	PLAYER hand draws (Rule 2) BANK hand draws or stands depending upon the value of the PLAYER's third card (Rule 5)
9 and 10	KING and 5	Both hands stand (Rule 1)
3 and ACE	2 and 4	PLAYER hand draws (Rule 2) BANK hand draws or stands depending upon the value of the PLAYER's third card (Rule 5)

Table 3

SECTION II

GAME OF OPPORTUNITIES

11 - Recognizing Opportunities

The great number of favorable opportunities a player will get in the game of Baccarat make it the most beatable Casino game (for the skilled player). Less skilled players will still have frequent advantages, but they will either not recognize many of them, or under-capitalize on them when they do.

An average Baccarat Shoe contains 80 decisions; seven are TIE's. The advantage during each of these 80 decisions will of course fluctuate between the player and the Casino. Over short-duration play sequences anything can happen. When the tables are turned against the Casino, specific outcomes in the decisions give the player an advantage, often a very big advantage. My analysis shows that a much of the time the player will have an advantage. I refer to these situations as opportunities. These frequent opportunities are the common streaks, patterns and trends in the outcomes found in a typical game of Baccarat. I know of no other Casino game that provides players with so many advantages.

But, what about a player's negative expectation or downside risk, recently referred to by some gaming authors as: cost to play, hourly rate of loss, or expected cost?

You can examine the game of Baccarat by crunching numbers in many ways, and call it any number of things, but none are of real use except to promote the latest analytical buzzwords.

What a player really has to know is:
1. Baccarat, dollar for dollar, offers the smallest Casino advantage.
2. Baccarat offers many player advantages, more than any other Casino game.
3. These player advantages can fluctuate, sometimes wildly in favor of the player.
4. When the advantage seems to be on the side of the Casino, a player can simply sit-out a few hands to see what develops.

In Baccarat, negative expectation has every-thing to do with the skill of the player and the number of player-advantages offered in a given Shoe. The greater the skill and the more advantages, the lower the negative ex-pectation.

Instead of a negative expectation focus, I prefer to address the upside, or the positive aspects of a given game. A game having a low Casino advantage, a large spread between the minimum and maximum bets, the ability to sit-out decisions, simplicity of the rules, num-ber of opportunities available and profit po-tential, and the skill required to play the game well are important factors to consider. None require any complicated mathematical analysis. Considering all the positive at-tributes, Baccarat remains unmatched.

In fact, the skilled Baccarat player enjoys a Net Positive Expectation (NPE). That is, dol-lar return based on the total dollars put in action will be positive; a net profit, rather than a net loss. The skilled player could actually lose more decisions than he or she wins, but still show a profit. Why? First, because the skilled player will recognize more opportunities. Second, they will make the most of these opportunities by being more aggressive. They will make larger bets when they have the advantage. It follows therefore that the greater the skill, the higher the NPE. Correspondingly, the more opportunities the greater the NPE. Of course the number of player-advantages in a given Shoe varies.

But, combined, player skill (opportunity recognition and a proper wagering strategy to take advantage of them) and the number of opportunities presented in a given Shoe, determine the NPE. Therefore, the NPE level one achieves is unique to each player. There is no single NPE that can be expressed for all players. Given at least good basic skills, including the ability to recognize opportunities, Baccarat will generally provide a positive outcome - a net positive expectation.

The dilemma is that some gaming authors like to rate or evaluate Casino games by developing a single comparative number. Unfortunately, any number in effect becomes meaningless, and more importantly misleading. The numbers do not always tell the real story. One does not need a number to tell the difference between a good meal and a bad one.

My overall play strategy is based upon many years of experience; thousands of hands of practice, and as many during actual Casino play, plus ongoing analysis of the results from hundreds of my scorecards.

Baccarat is a game of streaks and patterns that tend to be repetitive, and can be spotted by the skilled player. Armed with the knowledge of the kinds of typical trends in the outcomes, the skilled player is in a position to take advantage of them. There will be times when the expected trend does not materialize. But, there will also be many times when the expected trend is produced, a huge advantage for the player.

I classified the various types of outcomes in the decisions in a typical game of Baccarat into four broad categories:
1. Consecutive winning streaks
2. Repetitive patterns
3. Tie patterns
4. Random decisions

The first three categories of outcomes provide the player with the most opportunities. These opportunities are the streaks and patterns one finds in a typical game, and result in many advantages for the skilled practitioner. The question is, just what is the frequency of these opportunities?

> *"A player who wastes an opportunity is a Gamblers best friend."*
> *Anonymous Professional Gambler*

To determine the answer, I performed a statistical analysis against the outcomes in the decisions recorded on past scorecards to identify the frequency of outcomes from each of the first three classifications. The results provided reasonable data on the number of good opportunities one can expect to get in a typical game.

As a result of this analysis, I determined that there are four principle opportunity classifications:
1. Winning streaks of three or more consecutive decisions.
2. Repeating patterns of one or more repeats.
3. Repeating TIE patterns.
4. Consecutive TIE's.

They provide the principle basis for the techniques used to select what bets to make as the game progresses. Statistics on the results of this analysis, and examples from actual scorecards, are presented in the next Chapter.

12 - Opportunities Galore

At the risk of sounding like a statistician (an individual with his head in the refrigerator, his feet in the oven, and on the average feels quite comfortable), lets examine a few statistics that show the number of favorable opportunities a player can expect to get playing Baccarat.

The analysis is based on the use of the four opportunity classifications presented in Chapter 11, but with a few slight changes.
1. Winning streaks of four or more consecutive decisions.
2. Repeating patterns of two or more repeats.
3. Repeating TIE patterns.
4. Consecutive TIE's.

Notice that these opportunity classifications are more conservative. Instead of winning streaks of three or more decisions, I used four or more decisions for the first classification; instead of repeating patterns of one or more repeats, I used two or more repeats for the second. Using these more conservative classifications, I performed a statistical analysis on over 30,000 hands of actual short-duration play decisions. The results are summarized in Table 4, and provide a fairly conservative indication of the number of real opportunities you can expect to get in a typical Shoe of Baccarat.

Favorable Opportunities Per Shoe

# of Opportunities per Shoe	Percent (%) of Occurrences	Cumulative Occurrences Percent (%)
0 to 10	1	1
11 to 20	17	18
21 to 25	22	40
26 to 30	24	64
31 to 40	30	94
41 to 50	4	98
51 and Up	2	100

Table 4

The table shows that 82% of the Baccarat Shoes I played contained 21, or more, good opportunities. That is, I had an advantage over the Casino on at least 21 out of the 80 total decisions in the majority of Shoes (recall that an average Baccarat Shoe contains 80 decisions, seven of which are TIE's). Only 18% of the Shoes contained 20 or fewer favorable opportunities.

6% of the Shoes contained 41, or more, good opportunities. But, the really good news is that 46% contained 21 to 30 good opportunities, and 30% had 31 to 40. There is no other Casino game that offers this potential to win, and to win as frequently. I say potential to win because, as a player, you must be sufficiently skilled to garner the full benefits from the many advantages. Can you get the same number and frequency of good opportunities playing Blackjack or Craps?

Next, lets examine additional statistics that breakdown these favorable opportunities according to the original four broad opportunity classifications.

Winning Streaks

One of the most important reasons to play Baccarat, more than any other Casino game, is the frequent occurrence of various of consecutive winning streaks by both PLAYER and BANK. It is the first major opportunity classification: **Winning streaks of three or more consecutive decisions.** I have seen as many as 23 straight wins by BANK, and won one streak of 19 straight, as well as many dozens of streaks of 7 to 14 consecutive decisions. Consecutive winning streaks of three or more are fairly common.

Table 5 represents a summary of nearly 35,000 decisions, almost 500 Shoes, and shows the frequency of consecutive winning streaks of various lengths. This analysis of short-duration play shows that nearly 50% of the consecutive winning streak decisions will be streaks of three or more consecutive wins.

Based on these statistics, the following conclusions can be drawn:
1. Each successively longer consecutive win streak will occur approximately half as much as the previous one.
2. Some 48% of all consecutive winning streaks in a Shoe will be streaks of 3 or more.
3. Consecutive wins of more than 12 are fairly rare and will occur once or twice in approximately 125 Shoes.

Consecutive Winning Streak Summary

CONSECUTIVE WIN SEQUENCES	BANK OCCURRENCES	PLAYER OCCURENCES	TOTAL OCCURRENCES	TOTAL # OF HANDS
1	4,466	4,362	8,828	8,828
2	2,373	2,233	4,606	9,212
3	1,012	1,058	2,070	6,210
4	532	428	960	3,840
5	265	231	496	2,480
6	174	152	326	1,956
7	73	67	140	980
8	37	33	70	560
9	22	25	47	423
10	7	10	17	170
11	5	3	8	88
12	2	1	3	36
13	1	1	2	26
14	1	0	1	14
15 & Up	1	1	2	41
			TOTAL HANDS: 34,864	

Table 5

4. The outcomes in the decisions of a typical Shoe will likely contain:
   - 21 occurrences of single wins
   - 10 occurrences of double wins
   - 5-6 occurrences of 3 wins in a row
   - 3 occurrences of 4 wins in a row
   - 1 consecutive win streak 5,6,7,8,or 9

Obviously a player always wants to be wagering ON winning streaks, NOT against them (especially those of any length).

My most recent winning streak was 12 BANK wins in a row. The scorecard is shown in Figure 3; BANK wins 31 to 42. Notice that the streak was interrupted by a TIE decision after BANK win 40. Then two additional BANK wins followed, making the total winning streak 12. This is an important distinction; the winning streak is not ended by a TIE decision(s). Notice that BANK really dominated the Shoe, 46 wins for the BANK and only 27 for PLAYER. Also, there were two other very good BANK winning streaks of seven wins each in succession, BANK hands 17-23 and 24-30.

A disciplined approach to the game will ensure that you will be betting on, rather than against, any of these consecutive winning streaks. By that I mean establishing specific rules that are consistently applied to play.

The first rule, and most important rule for preventing a bad losing streak, is the **Switch-Stop (SS) Rule**. Switch sides when you have lost bets against three consecutive wins by PLAYER or BANK, or simply stop betting. Use this rule and you will never be on the wrong side of a long winning streak.

I am always amazed when a player loses bet after bet going against a winning streak; it is the mark of a very inexperienced player. Never ever chase in Baccarat, always **Go With the Flow**; the second, but most important rule for winning play.

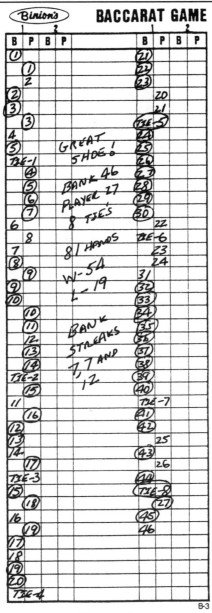

Figure 3

Another example of an excellent Shoe is transcribed in Figure 4. I was waiting for
friends to arrive for dinner at Bally's and
decided to play a few hands of Mini-Baccarat.
The Shoe was just about to begin and the
players were talking about how the BANK had
dominated the last few Shoes. Normally when I
do not cut the cards at the start of any new
Shoe, I bet PLAYER. But, because of these
comments, I decided to bet BANK; an excellent
move based on the results of the 27 hands I
played before leaving for dinner.

The BANK won the first nine hands. This was
followed a few hands later by another winning
streak of ten straight. Notice the two short
PLAYER streaks of three wins each between the
larger BANK winning streaks. Yes, I did have
some reservations about leaving, but I had
made my plans and stuck to them. It is always
good to quit after a great win!

B	P	B	P		B	P	B	P
①		z			⑮			
②			③		⑯			
③	⑩				⑰			
④		4		27 HANDS	TIE-1			
⑤			⑤	(1-TIE)	⑱			
⑥			⑥	WON 22	⑲			
⑦	⑪			OUT OF	⑳			
⑧	12			26				
⑨	⑬							
	1		⑭					

Figure 4

To summarize, the most profitable and easiest opportunities are these longer consecutive PLAYER and BANK winning streaks. So how can one be sure to wager on these opportunities? Answer: never wager against them! If you find yourself betting against any kind of consecutive winning streak, after two, or at most three straight losses, you must switch-over to the winning side, or quit betting. Doing so will ensure that you will never ever be wagering against any long winning streak, often the most profitable opportunity you may get (and the most dangerous to bet against). The Switch-Stop Rule will at worst save you a lot of money.

An even better answer to the previous question is to be wagering on these winning streaks from the very beginning. How? By looking for them. Having an awareness of the kinds of patterns that are typical, combined with a good scoring technique (and never wagering against the trend), it is more likely than not, you will be wagering with the streak.

Repetitive Patterns

Any combination of these consecutive winning streaks can also form repetitive patterns. This is the second major opportunity classi-fication: **Repeating patterns of one or more repeats.** These kinds of repetitive patterns in the decisions are excellent opportunities, particularly when they involve consecutive winning streaks of any great length, or when the pattern repeats several times. A typical Shoe will also include 3 to 4 of these re-petitive patterns.

There are many kinds of repetitive patterns. You must always be ready to consider them as possible decision outcomes. Let's review a few examples. Figure 5 shows another score-card transcribed from a recent trip; another big-money-maker! Notice again the dominance by BANK (45 wins to 29 for PLAYER) despite the early PLAYER winning streak of seven decisions.

B	P	B	P		B	P	B	P
(1)			12		(24)		(35)	
(2)	(9)				TIE-3		(36)	
(3)	(10)				(25)		(37)	
(4)	11				(26)			24
(TIE-1)	(12)				(27)		38	
(5)		13			(28)			25
(6)	(13)				(29)		(39)	
(7)		14			(30)		40	
(TIE-2)	(14)					18	(41)	
1		15				19	TIE-7	
	8		(15)		TIE-4		26	
2		(16)				20	(27)	
	(9)		(16)			(21)	(28)	
(3)	17				(TIE-5)	42		
4	18					(22)	(TIE-8)	
5	19					(23)	(29)	
(6)	(20)				31	43		
(7)	(21)				32	44		
	10		17		(33)	(TIE-9)		
(8)	(22)				(TIE-6)	(TIE-10)		
	11	(23)			(34)	45		

Figure 5

Again, when I do not cut the cards I always bet PLAYER to start a new Shoe (when I bet). In this case, PLAYER started with a natural 9 and I stayed with PLAYER for ten consecutive wagers, losing only the last one. Notice the two TIE's; the first TIE early in the Shoe was a TIE opportunity indicator (to be discussed later), so I placed bets on TIE and PLAYER for the next five decisions. The second TIE decision, after PLAYER win 7, paid-off handsomely.

After the PLAYER winning streak of seven straight, the decisions were somewhat choppy between progressively longer BANK winning streaks. I refer to these as dominant step-ups. These are fairly lopsided wins of generally ever increasing size. BANK wins 3 to 7 is five in a row, BANK wins 9 to 12 of four straight, then BANK wins 17 to 21 of five consecutive wins, and finally BANK wins 22 to 30, a great streak of nine straight wins. Starting with BANK win 3, PLAYER won only eight decisions out of the next 37 consecutive hands.

This pattern was followed by what I call dominant switches. The streak switched over to PLAYER which won six straight (PLAYER wins 18 to 23), and then switched back to BANK for a streak of seven straight wins (BANK wins 31 to 37). This was followed four decisions later by a nice matching pattern; three straight wins by BANK (39 to 41) and then three straight wins by PLAYER (26 to 28). These streaks were also characterized by TIE decision interruptions. I won 7 of the 10 TIE's in this Shoe by following the pattern. The consecutive TIE's, following BANK win 44, was the icing on the cake!

B	P	B	P		B	P	B	P
(1)	10				(26)	TIE-5		
(2)		(11)			(27)			20
(3)			(9)		(28)		(38)	
(4)		(12)			(29)			(21)
1		(13)				TIE-4		(TIE-6)
TIE-1	14					13		22
2		(15)			(30)		(39)	
3			10		(31)		(40)	
(5)		(16)			(32)		(41)	
(TIE-2)		(17)			(33)			23
(4)		(18)				14	(42)	
(5)		(19)				15		(24)
(6)		(20)				(16)		25
(6)		(21)			34		(43)	
7			11		(35)			(26)
7		(22)				17		27
(TIE-3)		(23)			(36)		TIE-7	
8		(24)				18		(28)
(9)			12		(37)		(TIE-8)	
(8)		(25)			(19)		44	

Figure 6

The transcribed scorecard in Figure 6 shows another typical repetitive pattern. The repetitive pattern essentially begins with PLAYER win 5. From BANK win 4 on, PLAYER wins a total of only eight decisions, and these are mostly single wins interspersed over 40 consecutive decisions. BANK won 30 of these decisions making the total score, after the pattern, a lopsided 33-13. Starting with BANK win 4, consecutive winning streaks by the BANK: 3, 3, 2, 4, 6, 3, 5 and 4.

In the end, BANK won 44 to PLAYER's 28. Notice also the TIE wins; I won 4 out the 8 TIE decisions. TIE patterns will be examined later in this Chapter.

Figure 7 is a transcription of another recent scorecard. The repeating PLAYER and BANK pairings are good examples of alternating short-win patterns: PLAYER wins 3 and 4, BANK wins 5 and 6, followed by another repeat (PLAYER wins 5 and 6, and BANK wins 7 and 8 which turned out to be a triple).

B	P	B	P	B	P	B	P
	1		7	19		27	
1			8	20		28	
2		10		21		29	
3		11				17	30
	2	12				18	28
4		9				19	29
	3	10				20	31
	4	11				21	32
TIE-1			12	22			33
5		13		23			30
6			13			22	34
TIE-2	14					23	31
TIE-3		14				24	TIE-5
	5	15				25	35
	6		15			26	36
7			16			27	32
8	16			24			37
9	17			25			
TIE-4	18			26			

Figure 7

Next, look at the consecutive winning streak by BANK of 6 straight (BANK wins 16 - 21), followed by a nearly matching PLAYER winning streak (PLAYER wins 17 - 21). These PLAYER and BANK winning streaks repeat again two decisions later: PLAYER wins 22 to 27 and BANK wins 24 to 30. These nearly matching and repetitive winning streaks are significant advantages for the skilled player.

Another example of repetitive pattern opportunities is shown in Figure 8.

B	P	B	P		B	P	B	P
1		(9)			(18)			25
	1	(10)			(19)			26
(2)			9		(18)	(29)		
	(2)		(10)			(19)		27
TIE-1			11		(20)		30	
(TIE-2)	11				(21)			(28)
	3		12		22			29
(TIE-3)	(12)					(20)		(30)
(3)			(13)			(21)		(31)
(4)			(14)		(23)			(32)
	4	(13)				22		(33)
	(5)	(14)			24			
	6	15				(23)		
(7)			15		(25)			
(8)		TIE-4			TIE-5			
5		(16)			26			
(6)		(17)			(27)			
(7)			16			(24)		
(8)			17		(28)			

Figure 8

Notice the matching repetitive alternating pair wins by the BANK and PLAYER; BANK wins 16 and 17, followed by PLAYER wins 16 and 17, then 18 and 19 for BANK, and 18 and 19 for PLAYER. PLAYER had two very nice winning streaks of five and six (PLAYER wins 4 to 8 and 28 to 33).

The transcribed scorecard in Figure 9 shows examples of repetitive matching consecutive winning streaks, and trend switches.

B	P	B	P		B	P	B	P
1			⑪		⑯			TIE-7
②			⑫		⑰		㉚	
TIE-1		⑩			⑱			26
	①		13		⑲		㉛	
3			⑭		⑳			27
	②		⑮		㉑		㉜	
	3		⑯		㉒			㉘
	④	11			㉓			29
4			⑰				23	㉝
⑤			⑱				24	30
	⑤		⑲		TIE-4		㉞	
	⑥		⑳		㉔		35	
	⑦	21			㉕			31
	8	12					25	㊱
⑥			㉒		TIE-5		㊲	
⑦		TIE-2			㉖			㉜
⑧		TIE-3			TIE-6			33
⑨		⑬			㉗		㊳	
	⑨	14			㉘		㊴	
	⑩	15			㉙			㉞ ㉟

Figure 9

Starting with PLAYER wins 5 to 8, followed immediately by a matching streak of four consecutive BANK wins (BANK wins 6 to 9), and a half repeat of four more consecutive PLAYER wins (wins 9 to 12). PLAYER then dominates with two other streaks of 4 and 5 straight wins (PLAYER wins 13 to 16, and 17 to 21). Shortly thereafter the trend switches; BANK dominates with a great winning streak of 11 straight (13 to 23), and a second smaller streak of 5 wins in a row (26 to 30).

Figure 10 shows an excellent example of a late repeat. It is a more sophisticated repeating pattern, and one that requires more concentration to pick-up on your scorecard. It involves repetitive patterns that reoccur later in the Shoe. I refer to these patterns as late repeats. Compare the decision sequences after TIE decision 4 with those after TIE decision 6; they are almost exactly the same. After TIE-4, BANK wins a single decision (win 24), followed by seven straight PLAYER wins (18 to 24), then for the next three decisions, a single win by BANK (25) and a double win by PLAYER (25 and 26).

This exact sequence repeats five decisions later following TIE-6, except for the last double PLAYER win (PLAYER wins only one decision: 35). It is always advisable to consider the outcomes of the decisions after a TIE; they could repeat. Applying the same pattern of outcomes after TIE-6, following the TIE-4 pattern, provided ten straight wins.

At other times, any random decision sequence could occur. But, with no other apparent pattern, why not bet that the previous sequence after TIE-4 will repeat after TIE-6.

B	P	B	P		B	P	B	P
	(1)		(9)			17		(29)
(1)	11				TIE-4			(30)
(TIE-1)	(12)				(24)			(31)
2			(10)			(18)		(32)
	(2)	(13)				(19)		(33)
(3)			11			20		(34)
4	(14)					(21)	(30)	
5	15					(22)		(35)
(TIE-2)	16				(TIE-5)	31		
	3	(17)				(23)		(36)
6			12			(24)	(32)	
	4	(18)			25		(33)	
	5	(19)				(25)	34	
	(6)	(20)				(26)	(35)	
(7)	(21)				26			TIE-7
(8)			13			(27)	(36)	
TIE-3			14		27			
	(7)	(22)			28			
	(8)		15		TIE-6			
(9)	23				(29)			
(10)			(16)			(28)		

Figure 10

Study your scorecard and look for these late repeats. This repeat did come fairly soon after the initial sequence; they do not always repeat this close together.

Another excellent repetitive pattern is single alternating decisions. These patterns are repetitive single wins going back and forth between PLAYER and BANK. Figure 11 is a good example of this common pattern.

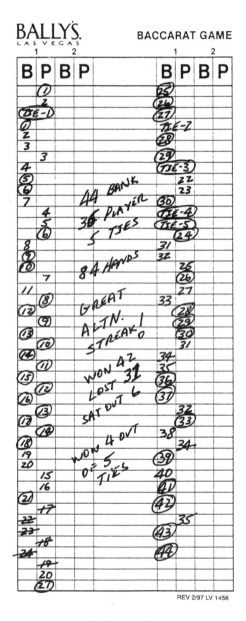

Figure 11

Figure 12 shows a repetitive pattern that I call back-to-back multiples. Beginning with BANK win 11: BANK wins three in a row; followed by four in a row for PLAYER; then a repeat of three in a row by BANK; followed by three straight PLAYER wins; then four in a row for BANK; followed by two straight for PLAYER; two straight by BANK; and another two in a row by PLAYER.

This sequence is excellent because I can make several large wagers on the second decision after each of the first BANK and PLAYER wins throughout the sequence. Based on the pattern, this is what I did on six occasions (PLAYER wins 13, 16 and 18, and BANK wins 15, 18, and 22).

Notice also that BANK had two winning streaks of six each (5 to 10 and 34 to 39). BANK dominated this Shoe 44 to 29.

Repetitive patterns come in all shapes and sizes. Keep a close eye on your scorecard and look for the various types of trends: repetitive matching win-streaks, alternating multiples, late repeats, trend switches, dominate step-ups and alternating short-wins.

TIE Opportunities

" *PLAYER shows a Natural 9, there will be no draw. Cards for the BANK please. BANK shows a Natural 9; TIE hand! Press or rearrange your wagers. $800 for Mr. H, $40 for the Dealers. Thank you for that bet Mr. H.* " I get paid quite often for my TIE wagers, and I also make TIE bets for the Dealers. The best part: TIE's pay 8 to 1!

B	P	B	P		B	P	B	P
(1)	(12)					(18)		26
2	(13)				(23)		(33)	
(3)			8			TIE-4		(27)
/			9			(19)	(34)	
(2)			(10)		24		35	
TIE-1			(11)			(20)	(36)	
	(4)	14				21	(37)	
3		(15)			25		(38)	
	5	(16)			(26)		(39)	
(4)			(12)		27			28
	(6)		(13)			22	(40)	
(5)			(14)			TIE-5	(41)	
TIE-2	(17)				(28)		(42)	
6	(18)					23	(43)	
7	(19)				(29)			29
(8)	20				30		(44)	
(9)		15			(31)			
(10)		(16)				24		
	7	21			(25)			
TIE-3	(22)				TIE-6			
(11)			(17)		(32)			

Figure 12

Wagering on TIE's must be a standard bet in certain spot-betting situations. This is of course contrary to the advice of most of the so-called experts (who are therefore less sophisticated Baccarat players). It is true that there is a high Casino advantage on TIE's (approximately 14%), but when TIE's repeat and you win them, the Casino advantage is not relevant.

My analysis of thousands of hands of short-duration play shows that the number of hands played between TIE's is often quite small, and there can be a repetitive pattern to them. A typical Baccarat Shoe will contain 6 or 7 TIE's. But when there are 10 to 15 TIE's in a Shoe, TIE's will often occur in bunches, and there will be more pattern TIE decisions.

In all Casino games you are looking to exploit opportunities; Tie-Bet opportunities are one of the most profitable. But, you must be able to quickly recognize them to take full advantage of them. Use the following Opportunity Indicators (OI's) as a guide:
1. One or more TIE decisions early in the Shoe.
2. Multiple TIE decisions with only one to four decisions between TIE occurrences.
3. Consecutive TIE decisions.

These OI's, more often than not, result in true Tie-Bet opportunities. With a payoff of 8 to 1, they are too profitable to pass-up. Watch your scorecard for these OI's, and bet TIE accordingly.

Players have two major advantages associated with TIE's: **Repeating TIE patterns and Consecutive TIE's,** the third and fourth major opportunity classifications.

Repeating TIE Patterns

Repeating TIE patterns are TIE decisions that repeat again and again within a fairly fixed and consistent number of decisions. The number of decisions between each repeating TIE can be just a few or many.

Table 6 contains a separate statistical breakdown for the opportunities you can expect to get in both TIE-RICH and non-TIE-RICH (Normal) Shoes. I refer to Baccarat Shoes that contain a lot more TIE's than the normal seven or less as TIE-RICH Shoes. TIE-RICH Shoes contain an average of 11 TIE's; about one in five Shoes will be TIE-RICH.

TIE Pattern Opportunities

# of Hands Between TIE's	Occurrences in Percent (%)			
	TIE-Rich	Cum. %	Normal	Cum. %
0 to 2	37	37	17	17
3 to 4	17	54	8	25
5 to 7	21	75	13	38
8 & Up	25	100	62	100

Table 6

Referring to Table 6, note the statistical comparison between the TIE-RICH Shoes and the Normal Shoes. TIE's often occur in bunches, particularly in TIE-RICH Shoes. That is, the number of hands between TIE's is quite small.

The data shows that after a TIE there is a 75% probability that another TIE will occur within the next eight hands in TIE-RICH Shoes. There is even a 38% probability in Normal Shoes that another TIE will occur within the next eight decisions. For TIE-RICH Shoes, there is a 54% probability that there will be another TIE within the next five hands, more than a 50/50 proposition that pays 8 to 1!

These are excellent spot-betting situations, even though such bets have a high Casino advantage.

The opportunities in TIE-RICH Shoes for 0 to 2 decisions between TIE's are more than twice as good as Normal Shoes, 37% versus 17%. For 0 to 4 decisions between TIE's, it is 54% versus 25%. The player has a huge advantage in TIE-RICH Shoes. Of course, you will not know if a particular Shoe is TIE-RICH or not. Use the OI's previously presented and bet accordingly. Proper TIE wagering methods will be covered in detail later.

During a recent trip to Las Vegas, I played seven Shoes. Four of the seven contained Tie-Bet OI's, and all four were true opportunities. I won 38 out of the 45 total TIE decisions in these Shoes. One Shoe contained an amazing run of 5 TIE decisions in a row, very unusual and very profitable. A five-dollar parlay would provide a profit of $29,155 after the fourth TIE bet win. The fifth bet would be the table maximum of either $5,000 or $10,000. Consecutive TIE decisions, and the occasional triple, are more typical.

This sequence may have been somewhat unusual, but you will generally find true Tie-Bet opportunities in about one-third of the Baccarat Shoes you will play.

Consecutive TIE's

Again referring to Table 6, you are probably asking why list *0-2* in the *# of Hands Between TIE's* column; how can you have zero hands between TIE's? The answer is consecutive TIE's.

I have seen four in a row twice, and won five in a row once. Consecutive TIE's is the fourth major opportunity classification.

Lets review a few examples of the various types of TIE opportunities. Figure 13 is a transcribed scorecard from my first trip to Kansas City. It contains 15 TIE decisions. I won 11 based on recognizing TIE pattern opportunities, and applying my rules for wagering on them.

B	P	B	P		B	P	B	P
1			5		(20)			(19)
(2)			(6)		21		(32)	
	1		7				13	33
3		12			22		(34)	
(4)			TIE-6		(TIE-10)		(35)	
TIE-1		13			(23)		(36)	
5		(14)			(24)			20
(6)			(8)		(25)			21
	2		(9)			14	(37)	
(TIE-2)		(TIE-7)				15	(38)	
(7)			(10)			(16)	39	
(TIE-3)			(11)		(26)			TIE-12
(TIE-4)		15			(27)		(40)	
(8)		(16)			(28)			(TIE-13)
(9)		(17)			TIE-11		(41)	
(TIE-5)		(18)				17	(TIE-14)	
	3	(TIE-8)			29			22
	4	(19)			(30)			(23) 24
10			12			18	42	
(11)			(TIE-9)		31			(TIE-15)

Figure 13

Notice the number of decisions between the
first five TIE's. The first TIE decision came
early in the Shoe, so I looked for additional
TIE decisions to come with only a few hands
between them. The second TIE appeared four
decisions later, TIE-3 only two decisions
later, TIE-4 was a consecutive TIE, and TIE-5
three decisions thereafter. I missed TIE-6,
but made the next four TIE's: TIE-7, 8, 9,
and 10. I also missed TIE 11 and 12, but won
all the rest: TIE-13, 14, and 15, which was
the last hand of the Shoe. First and last decision TIE's are fairly common. I routinely
bet TIE on both the first and last decisions
of every Shoe.

There were also good winning streaks for
BANK. BANK had eight separate winning
streaks: two of 4 decisions in a row, three
triples, and three of 5 straight decisions.

Figure 14 is an actual scorecard. It contains
15 TIE decisions, another great win! Notice
the bunched TIE decisions, and the two pairs
of consecutive TIE's. There was also a TIE on
the last hand of the Shoe, and nearly a TIE
on the first hand. The early TIE on the second decision was a good TIE indicator, so I
bet TIE for the next six decisions. Even
though another TIE did not occur until the
tenth decision, I was convinced that this
would be a good TIE Shoe. As it turned out,
the Shoe was great, very TIE-RICH.

Referring to Figure 14, TIE-3 occurred on the
thirteenth decision, followed by TIE-4 five
decisions later, TIE-5 after six more hands,
TIE-6 after two more decisions, TIE-7 after
five more hands, TIE-8 seven decisions later,
TIE-9 after four more decisions, and TIE-10
four hands later.

I missed TIE-11, but won TIE-12, the first consecutive TIE. TIE-13 came after five more decisions, and TIE-14 was the second consecutive TIE. Seven hands later, I won TIE-15, the last hand of the Shoe. I won 13 out of the 15 total TIE decisions; outstanding!

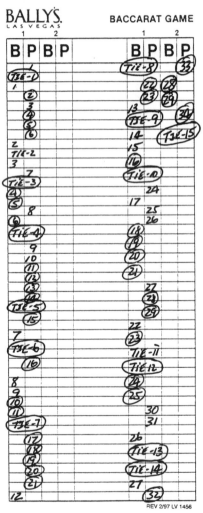

Figure 14

The transcribed scorecard in Figure 15 is another example of a great TIE Shoe. Notice the
two pairs of consecutive TIE's (one double
and one triple), particularly the double
which occurred as the first two decisions of
the Shoe. What a great way to start! I won 8
out of the 12 total TIE decisions.

BANK also won eleven out of the first twelve
non-TIE decisions. After a PLAYER win of
three in a row and a single win by each, BANK
won five straight (wins 13 to 17). Then the
trend really switched; PLAYER won four
straight (wins 6 to 9), then eight in a row
(wins 11 to 18), followed by a winning streak
of nine in a row (wins 19 to 27), and finally
seven straight wins (28 to 34). BANK ended on
a run of six straight (wins 23 to 28).

The consecutive winning streaks, plus the
TIE's, made this one of the best Shoes for
number of player opportunities anyone could
hope to get. I won 53 of the 80 total decisions. The actual number of good opportunities in this Shoe was over 60, a huge advantage for the skilled player.

Figure 16 shows that one can get TIE opportunities in a normal (non-TIE-RICH) Shoe. This
Shoe had only 6 TIE's, but it contained both
first-hand and last-hand TIE's. The TIE decisions are also nearly perfectly patterned.
The number of decisions between TIE-1 and
TIE-2 is 12. I routinely check the number of
decisions between TIE's. In this case, bet
that there will be another TIE 11 to 13 decisions later. I give myself a plus or minus
one decision leeway for next TIE wagers following the repetitive pattern. TIE-3 occurred
12 decisions later; TIE-4 13 decisions later;
and TIE-5, also 13 decisions later.

B	P	B	P		B	P	B	P
TIE-1	(16)					(22)		35
TIE-2	(17)					(23)		36
(1)			6		TIE-9			(37)
(2)			7			(24)		(38)
(3)			(8)			(25)	30	
(4)			(9)			(26)		
(5)		18				(27)		
TIE-3			10		22			
(6)		(19)				(28)		
	1		(11)		TIE-10			
(7)			12			29		
(8)			(13)		TIE-11			
(9)			(14)			30		
(10)			(15)			(31)		
(11)			(16)			(32)		
	2		(17)			(33)		
	3		(18)			(34)		
	(4)	TIE-6			23			
12		(TIE-7)			24			
	5	(TIE-8)			(25)			
13		20			(26)			
(14)		21			TIE-12			
TIE-4		19			(27)			
15		(20)			(28)			
(TIE-5)		(21)			(29)			

Figure 15

Pattern TIE's do not have to be closely bunched. Pay attention to the number of decisions between TIE's, and consider making a bet that the number of decisions between TIE's will be nearly the same.

B	P	B	P		B	P	B	P
TIE-1	13				15	28		
1			7		16			29
2		14			17	29		
3			8		18			30
	1	15			19	31		
4		TIE-3			20	32		
	2	16			21			31
	3	17			22	33		
5		18			23			32
6			9		23		34	
7			10		24	35		
8			11		TIE-5	36		
9			12		25			33
TIE-2	19				24		TIE-6	
10		20			25			
11		21			26			
	4		13		26			
	5	22			27			
	6	TIE-4			27			
12			14		28			

Figure 16

First and Last TIE's

One other type of repetitive TIE pattern is
first decision and last decision TIE's. They
are quite common in TIE-RICH Shoes, but are
also found in Normal Shoes, as some of the
examples have shown. I routinely make TIE wagers on the first hand and last hand of every
Shoe. My last trip to Las Vegas all four
Shoes I played had both first and last TIE
decisions; I won all 8.

Figure 17 is a scorecard showing that first and last TIE's, as well as consecutive TIE's, can be found even in Shoes with the normal seven or less total TIE's.

B	P	B	P		B	P	B	P
TIE-1		(11)				26	(42)	
1		12			TIE-5	43		
	(2)		(12)			27		(37)
(2)			13			(28)		38
	(3)	13				(29)	(44)	
(3)			(14)		30		(45)	
	(4)		(15)		31			(39)
	5		(16)		(32)		TIE-6	
4			(17)			30	TIE-7	
TIE-2			(18)		33			
	(6)	14				(31)		
TIE-3		(19)			34			
TIE-4		(20)				(32)		
(5)		(21)			(35)			
6		15				(33)		
(7)		16			(36)			
(8)		(17)			37			
(9)		(18)			38			
	7	(19)				34		
(10)			22		(39)			
	8	(23)			(40)			
	9	(24)				35		
	(10)	(25)			(41)			
11		20				36		

Figure 17

Also notice the three pairs of alternating single wins at the start of the Shoe. Later there was a second BANK and PLAYER alternating single win pattern (PLAYER wins 30 to 32 and BANK wins 33 to 36). There were two good matching winning streaks for BANK and PLAYER, BANK wins 5 to 9, and PLAYER wins 14 to 18.

TIE Wrap-UP

The best player advantages are associated with TIE pattern opportunities. Winning TIE wagers pay 8 to 1, so the potential for big and quick profits is a danger to the Casino.

However, the average Baccarat Shoe will contain only 7 TIE decisions out of the average of 80 total decisions. But, there will also be Shoes that contain a lot more TIE's, the TIE-RICH Shoes. Recall that TIE-RICH Shoes contain an average of 11 TIE's. They provide some of the best possible opportunities a player can get, nearly a sure thing, or at least the closest you will ever get in any Casino game.

If you bet $10 on TIE on every hand of the Shoe, the break-even point is approximately 9 TIE's. In an 80 hand Shoe, you would lose $710 on the non-TIE decisions, but win $720 on the 9 TIE wins. In an 80 hand Shoe with 14 TIE's, you would win $1120 on the TIE's and lose $660 on the non-TIE's, for a net gain of $460.

I am not advocating a TIE bet on every single decision of a Shoe. I am simply illustrating the fact that when you have more than the usual number of TIE's, you can make money.

However, by betting on TIE's selectively, a lot more money will be made. That is, using the TIE indicators look for potential patterns and bet on them. Later, a few basic rules will be established to assist you take full advantage of these opportunities.

But, how do you know the Shoe will contain a lot of TIE's? The answer: you do not need to know. Potential TIE opportunities get played automatically, due to the standard rules established for pattern TIE opportunities.

Take advantage of these 8 to 1 payoff opportunities. You will be the envy of everyone at the Baccarat table. No one will be playing them, and more importantly, winning TIE's like you. Of course, they will think it is just luck, but we know otherwise!

Conclusion

The normal Casino advantage is based on the long haul, many hundreds of playing hours. We take our shot at the Casino's money over relatively short time periods, and there are plenty of opportunities to exploit during these brief encounters. These opportunities are the frequent appearance of various streaks, patterns and trends. A player must become very familiar with them to take full advantage of these potential opportunities. Keep your scorecards neat and tidy, you will want to save them for further study.

The examples of these frequent and favorable opportunities are the main categories. Learn them well and you will be on your way to becoming a successful Baccarat player. Practice and experience are the best teachers.

13 - The Shoe With Few Opportunities

Of course the most difficult Shoes to play are those with very few favorable opportunities. These Shoes are characterized by the absence of any decent consecutive winning streaks (of any length), and the lack of repetitive patterns.

The scorecard in Figure 18 is a good example of a Shoe with fewer than the average 20 favorable opportunities. Notice that several bets were skipped (indicated by the recorded decision number crossed-out). This Shoe had one pair of consecutive TIE's and only two short consecutive BANK winning streaks of four straight wins each. BANK hands 20 through 24, and 37 to 40. This Shoe had less than 10 good opportunities.

Recall the four primary decision outcome classifications:
1. Consecutive winning streaks
2. Repetitive patterns
3. Tie patterns
4. Random decisions

The first three classifications contain the best player opportunities. The fourth classification, Random Decision Outcomes (RDO's), are very difficult to win. Therefore, play should be defensive; players must bet the minimum or sit-out a few hands.

B	P	B	P		B	P	B	P
(TIE-1)			(9)			18		(27)
	(1)		10			19		28
1			11					
	2	13						
(2)			12		(24)		(36)	
3			(13)		(25)		(37)	
	3	14				20	(38)	
(4)		(14)			TIE-5		(39)	
(5)		(15)				21		29
6		15				22	TIE-6	
	(4)	TIE-3			20̶		(TIE-7)	
	5	16				23	(40)	
TIE-2			16		2̶7̶		41	
	6	(TIE-4)			2̶8̶			
(7)		(17)			2̶4̶			
(8)		(18)			2̶9̶			
	7	19				2̶5̶		
9			17		3̶0̶			
(10)		(20)			3̶1̶			
	8	(21)			3̶2̶			
(11)		(22)				(26)		
(12)		23			(33)			
					(34)			
					35			

Figure 18

The skillful player still has an important advantage; he or she does NOT have to make a bet on every decision. When there are only a few favorable opportunities, wait until a good one is presented before making a bet.

Alternatively, quit and try again later. There will be other Shoes that will likely offer many more advantages.

When opportunities are few and far between, conserve your bankroll. Bet the minimum, or better yet, don't bet at all! Smart play often means no-play!

14 - Section Review and Summary

The four primary decision outcome classifications are:
1. Consecutive winning streaks
2. Repetitive patterns
3. Tie patterns
4. Random decisions

The first three classifications provide the best player opportunities and were further broken down into the four main favorable opportunity categories:
1. Winning streaks of three or more consecutive decisions.
2. Repeating patterns of one or more repeats.
3. Repeating TIE patterns.
4. Consecutive TIE's.

82% of the Baccarat Shoes you play will contain 21 or more excellent opportunities. Six percent will contain 41, or more good opportunities; 46% will contain 21 to 30; and 30% will have between 31 and 40. Only about 18% of the Shoes you play will contain 20 or fewer favorable opportunities. There is no other Casino game that provides so many player advantages.

A disciplined approach to the game will ensure that you make the most from these frequent advantages. The skilled player establishes a set of specific guidelines and rules that are consistently applied to their play.

Guidelines & Rules for Disciplined Play:

1. Switch sides when you have lost three con- secutive bets against three straight wins by PLAYER or BANK, or simply stop betting. This is the Switch-Stop (SS) Rule. It will prevent you from ever getting on the wrong side of a long consecutive winning streak.
2. Go With the Flow. Never ever bet against a consecutive winning streak in Baccarat.
3. Study and learn the typical streaks, pat- terns and trends that are likely to occur. When you recognize them, bet on them to continue or repeat.
4. Watch for Repetitive TIE pattern opportu- nities; TIE's can occur in bunches and in repetitive patterns.
5. Bet TIE after a TIE; consecutive TIE's are fairly common.
6. Bet TIE on the first and last decisions of the Shoe.
7. Consider betting early and late TIE's, the first and last four decisions of the Shoe.
8. When in doubt, bet the minimum, or don't bet at all. Skip a few bets and bet only when there is a good opportunity.

Wrap-Up

Study and re-study the examples of the vari- ous types of streaks and patterns. They may not always present themselves in the same manner, and of course, there are many other possibilities. But, an educated guess, based upon knowledge and experience, is a whole lot better than just a guess.

Lesson three is next: making the Casino's money your money.

SECTION III

TACTICS & STRATEGIES

15 - The Power Baccarat 2 Formula

The most frequent questions I receive essentially have one common theme: What *System* provides the best chance of winning? But, what does the word *system* mean?

Webster defines system as an organized set of principles that are used to form a procedure. In Casino gaming, there are no simple, easy, or magic formulas. There are only combinations of principles forming procedures, which may provide a winning opportunity over short periods of time.

And, there are no legal systems that will defeat the Casino over long periods of continuous play. In the short-run, the advantage shifts back and forth. The Casino may enjoy an advantage for a time, and then the decision patterns may favor the player.

The development of a winning system can take many years of trial and error. In the process of developing a system that I could rely upon and be comfortable with, I found my own basic gaming philosophy was emerging. I was finally seeing a bigger picture, an overall approach that ultimately resulted in the development of **POWER BACCARAT**.

A Recipe for Success

A basic gaming philosophy is a set of principles, beliefs and practices, which form the
basis for how an individual plays a given
game. When combined with realistic expecta-
tions, reasonable skill, play discipline and
mental toughness, a pretty formidable game
plan emerges. But it starts with a player's
gaming philosophy. Ones philosophy must compliment his or her skill, bankroll and expec-
tations.

Over the years, I have developed a philosophy
about Casino gaming in general, and Baccarat
in particular. Any player serious about winning should do likewise. The best way is to
lay it out on paper.

Think about what games you play, and why you
play them, as opposed to others that you do
not play. How do you play the games? What are
your beliefs about gaming in general, as well
as the specific games you play? Are your beliefs accurate, or upon further examination,
do you find that you actually have some misconceptions or erroneous information?

Do you enjoy the games you play? Are you a
skilled player? How often do you practice?
How often do you win or lose? What steps do
you think you need to take to win more often?
Upon self-examination, what areas of play do
you need to work on to get better? Do you
play to win, or do you play not to lose? Are
you conservative or aggressive? What are your
best gaming attributes? What other attributes
would you like to acquire? These are just a
few of the questions that you must answer to
define your individual philosophy.

After formalizing my gaming philosophy, I found it was a perfect match for the game of Baccarat. Baccarat met or exceeded each of the attributes I felt were important to be successful. The key principles, beliefs and practices that comprise my gaming philosophy are:

1. Play games that offer the best opportunity to win.
2. Simple is better; play games that are easy to learn.
3. Have fun and accept the challenge.
4. Use short duration play sequences.
5. Play games that do not require a bet on each and every decision.
6. Play games that are widely available, and where the rules are the same in all Casinos.
7. Play games that can be played with a smallish bankroll and have low minimums.
8. Play games that are fairly easy to master.
9. Play games that compliment ones style of play.
10. Practice-perfected game plans work.

As shown in the graphic, a basic gaming philosophy is the foundation for each of the other building blocks, which together, form the basis for a successful game plan.

On top of the foundation is the next level: knowledge and experience. A player must take the time to learn the game and gain needed experience.

The next level contains the intangibles: discipline and mental toughness. Winning requires self-confidence, trust in a well-conceived game plan and the mental toughness to stay with it.

The top level is the game plan itself, POWER BACCARAT 2.

GAME PLAN
DISCIPLINE & MENTAL TOUGHNESS
KNOWLEDGE & EXPERIENCE
GAMING PHILOSOPHY

A Winning System – POWER BACCARAT 2

The player has the option to chose what games to play, when to play, what to bet on and how much to bet, and when to quit.

Your greatest weapon against the Casino is to put together these options within a systematic method of play.

A winning system will keep a player in the game long enough to get a favorable opportunity; outcomes in the decisions that favor the player.

Getting the best of it during these situations requires an organized, pre-planned, practice-perfected method of play. Along the way, you will win a few and lose a few, while waiting for those favorable opportunities.

I use the word *Power* in the phrase Power Baccarat 2 to describe my overall method of playing the game. I want to carefully control how I play. This requires a plan of attack that considers all the important variables, and yet has built-in contingencies that allow for midstream adjustments based on the outcomes of the decisions as the game progresses.

I have described my plan like that of the football team who exploits its opponent's weaknesses, and effectively utilizes its most potent scoring or defensive weapons.

Their game plan also incorporates ongoing measurement and assessment of its effectiveness allowing for adjustments. Coaches located above the field of play may direct a change in offensive or defensive alignments to secure the most advantageous individual player match-ups; forcing a slower Linebacker to cover a Back for example. Both teams are constantly looking for ways to gain an edge. If properly conceived, the plan remains in affect, only minor adjustments are necessary as the game is played.

This is the concept I apply to playing Baccarat. I call it Power Baccarat 2. Power Baccarat 2 doesn't guarantee a winning performance, but it does provide the best possible chance to win.

The Power Baccarat 2 formula is:
Bet Selection Methods + Money Management Systems + Play Discipline + Hit'em & Run

Individually, the elements are:
Part 1: Bet Selection Methods - what to bet on and when.
Part 2: Money Management Systems - how much to bet.
Part 3: Play Discipline - playing with a practice-perfected plan.
Part 4: Hit'em & Run - mental toughness, knowing yourself and picking the right spots.

There are no methods that will guarantee you'll beat the Casino. However, choosing what to bet on, when to bet, and how much can be pre-determined. That is, your decisions can be based on the current trend of the cards, and matched to the most appropriate Bet Selection Method and Money Management System.

A menu, of pre-planned Bet Selection Methods and Money Management Systems must be at your fingertips. Bet Selection Methods answer the *what to bet on and when* questions. Money Management Systems answer the *how much* question.

If you execute Part 1 of the Power Baccarat 2 formula well, but do not take advantage of the situation by wagering enough money, you are not taking your best shot at the Casino. It is like playing for a field goal instead of a touchdown. And, if you do poorly with Part 1 and bet too much, you will lose too much of your Bankroll to take advantage of a good opportunity when it comes.

Part 3 of the Power Baccarat 2 formula is Play Discipline, another very important part of the formula. Discipline is establishing a game plan, perfecting it and sticking to it.

Part 4, is Hit'em & Run; strategies that will ensure you make the best of it, and when circumstances dictate, you quickly retreat.

The proper strategy calls for short-duration play, aggressively increasing the size of ones bets when winning (offensive play), and when losing, cutting back to conserve your bankroll (defensive play).

> *"When schemes are laid in advance, it is surprising how often the circumstances fit in with them."*
> *William Osler*

The key ingredient to success is making the most timely and optimal adjustments, based upon the trends in the outcomes of the cards. Your ability to do this will improve as you gain experience.

This Section will examine each of the individual elements of the Power Baccarat 2 formula, and more importantly, show how they fit together to form a winning game plan - **Power Baccarat 2!**

16 - Bet Selection Methods

Bet Selection, is the process for determining what bets to make and when to make them. The process of bet selection is part science and part art. Part science because one must have knowledge of the kinds of opportunities available; the streaks, patterns and trends in the decision outcomes common in a typical game of Baccarat. Part art because one has to quickly recognize these opportunities. This requires experience, intuition and a feel for the flow of the game.

It takes experience because it based upon spotting and anticipating opportunities. If you cannot spot most of them, and do so quickly, you will be unsuccessful.

The skilled player is able to read his or her scorecard. That is, evaluate the outcomes of past recorded decisions, assess possible patterns and trends in the outcomes, determine the most probable pattern for future outcomes, choose the applicable Bet Selection Method, and evaluate the actual results. This process is repeated after each decision.

Bet Selection is not guessing. It is the process of choosing what bets to make from several possible alternatives based upon the flow of the game, the patterns and trends in previous decision outcomes.

At first, a good deal of concentration is required. With practice and experience, this process becomes automatic, and more importantly, results in more wins.

Of course it is necessary to know each of the common kinds of decision outcomes, particularly those that offer the best opportunities for the player.

Additionally, it is necessary to develop a simple scoring system to record the outcomes of the decisions as the game progresses. Scoring is important because one must constantly study and evaluate past decisions looking for potential future opportunities.

In Baccarat, there are five different bets that can be made:
- BANK (by itself)
- PLAYER (by itself)
- BANK and TIE (both)
- PLAYER and TIE (both)
- TIE (by itself)

Selecting the best bets to make at the right time is the objective of the Bet Selection Process. Success means winning more hands than you lose. But, you could win more hands than you lose, and still lose money, if you bet too much on losing decisions. On the other hand, you could lose more hands, and still win money by wagering aggressively when you have the advantage.

In the previous Section the various types of outcomes were classified and presented, along with several examples illustrating the many advantages a player will get in a typical game.

As the game proceeds, patterns and trends in the outcomes will become apparent. An early domination by the PLAYER or BANK, a winning streak or repetitive pattern, or a pattern of TIE's can easily be observed as the outcomes are recorded on your scorecard.

As the patterns and trends appear and change, individual Bet Selection Methods must be selected, and adjustments made as required. By quickly studying recorded past decisions, determine what potential pattern or trend is expected for the next few hands. However, this decision must not be fixed. The outcome of the next hand, and each succeeding hand, may call for a change.

Suppose your scorecard showed PLAYER to be significantly ahead of BANK in total number of wins, and that BANK has won very few consecutive decisions. Following a single win by BANK, PLAYER has won the last three decisions. You could determine that either:
1. PLAYER will continue to dominate BANK and you will bet on the PLAYER winning streak to continue.
2. BANK will win the next decision followed by three more PLAYER wins; a repeat of the last four decisions.
3. You remain cautious, but feel a turnaround for the BANK is probable.

Suppose, based on the trend, you select alternative 2, and bet accordingly. If BANK wins, you stick with your plan to bet PLAYER on the next decision, looking for a total of three consecutive PLAYER wins. If BANK loses, you must again evaluate the possible alternatives.

This process of reviewing your scorecard, assessing possible patterns and trends in the outcomes, deciding on the most probable pattern, choosing the applicable Bet Selection Method, and evaluating results, is the Bet Selection process.

Recall there are four primary decision outcome classifications:
1. Consecutive winning streaks
2. Repetitive patterns
3. Tie patterns
4. Random decisions

I use a total of twelve Bet Selection Methods to play them. The first three classifications contain the best player opportunities. A typical Shoe will contain at least 21 opportunities as a result of these three classifications. My analysis indicates that 82% of Shoes will contain 21, or more, good wagering opportunities (out of the 80 decisions in an average Shoe); 54% will have 26 to 40 opportunities. Play must be offensive because the player has the advantage.

The fourth outcome classification, Random Decision Outcomes (RDO's), favor the Casino, and are of course the most difficult to play. During such occasions, overall play is defensive in nature, and therefore players must bet the minimum or sit-out a few hands. Smart play often means no-play, but at most, low play!

Every Baccarat Shoe will contain a mixture of each of these decision outcomes. Obviously, the greater the frequency of the first three, the more opportunities for the player.

The three general classifications offering the best player opportunities, are further broken down into four specific categories:
1. Winning streaks of three or more consecutive decisions
2. Repeating patterns of one or more repeats
3. Pattern TIE Repeats
4. Consecutive TIE's

Based on these four categories, I established seven different Bet Selection Methods. Each method is associated with at least one of the categories, and they are of course offensive in nature.

I also established five additional Bet Selection Methods for playing RDO's: four neutrals, and one negative. The four neutral methods cover specific situations, and those outcomes that do not fit precisely within any of the categories. I also use them as a check-and-balance in my decision process for selecting another method.

As you can see, the process of selecting what bets to make is very deliberate and highly organized. Success requires a good scoring technique, and both knowledge and experience. Bet Selection is a deductive and intuitive reasoning process; part science and part art. Guessing is how the amateurs play! Let's examine each of the twelve Bet Selection Methods.

1. Same As Last Decision

Same As Last Decision means to bet the same on the next decision as the winning outcome on the previous decision. If BANK won the last hand, bet BANK, if PLAYER won, bet PLAYER. Continue to bet that the winner of the previous decision will win again until a pre-determined number of winning decisions is reached, or until a loss occurs. Then re-evaluate the trend and select the best option.

Because consecutive winning streak patterns are so favorable, players must take full advantage of them by being aggressive. That is, making the right bets at the right times must be complimented by aggressive increases in the size of successive winning wagers. Of course the term aggressive is relative. It means that one must be aggressive within the limits of their bankroll and individual styles of play.

For example, suppose BANK has won three straight decisions, and your last bet was a losing one on PLAYER. My rules require me to stop betting, or switch sides, in this case making a bet on BANK. This rule ensures I will never be betting against a winning streak, the worst possible circumstance for any Baccarat player. Consecutive winning streaks of 7 to 10 wins in a row are not uncommon. In this example, a winning streak of three or more consecutive decisions by BANK must be considered a good opportunity.

Continuing with this winning streak scenario (BANK has won the last three decisions), bet BANK on the next decision. If BANK wins, it would be the fourth straight win. Continue to bet BANK until PLAYER wins, then reassess the trend. A matching win streak on PLAYER is possible, or BANK could continue to win. Consider future outcome alternatives both in the context of the overall flow of the Shoe, and the last dozen or so decisions. Study your scorecard and remain focused.

Let us suppose that BANK won a total of eight straight decisions, five in a row since switching over to BANK. The bets made on BANK for a $5 player (being aggressive after a win) would typically look like this for the five consecutive wins: $5, $10, $10, $15, $20 and a $10 last bet losing to PLAYER. These six wagers produced a net gain of $50, more than twice the gain if a flat bet of $5 is made on each decision.

Obviously, selecting the correct bets is the first step, but making the most from the opportunity also requires an aggressive wagering approach. To be successful one needs to master both skills.

Refer to Figures 3, 4 and 5 in Chapter 12. These scorecards contain examples of consecutive winning streaks bet using this Bet Selection Method. It is the most common method and the one that will produce your largest wins.

2. Opposite Last Decision

Opposite Last Decision means to bet the opposite of the outcome of the previous decision. If PLAYER won the last hand, bet BANK. If BANK won the previous hand, bet PLAYER.

This Bet Selection Method is used along with the first method, Same As Last Decision, to play the second opportunity classification *Repeating Patterns of one or more Repeats*. Recall that opportunities from this classification can sometimes be just as profitable as consecutive winning streak patterns. These outcomes form a specific pattern, and the exact same pattern of outcomes repeats, one or more times (occasionally many more times). The pattern could be P-B-P-B-P-B-P-B (where P is a PLAYER win and B is a BANK win); three repeats of single alternating wins by PLAYER and BANK. I have seen as many as seven repeats of this pattern. Another example pattern would be B-B-P-B-B-P-B-B-P-B-B-P; three repeats of a double BANK win followed by a single PLAYER win. As you can see these repetitive patterns can be outstanding opportunities, particularly when they repeat several times.

In addition to these kinds short alternating win patterns, there are many other repetitive patterns. There are patterns of short alternating win streaks such as four BANK wins followed by four PLAYER wins, and a repeat or partial repeat. It is important to note that even if the pattern does not fully repeat, a partial one can still be very profitable.

Additionally, I always examine the outcomes of the decisions that occur after TIE's. Occasionally the pattern of decisions following a TIE repeats after another TIE. I refer to these as late repeats. But, they are not so easy to spot, especially when the repeat is much later in the Shoe.

The Bet Selection Methods to use are a combination of Same as Last Decision and Opposite Last Decision depending on the repeating pattern of decisions you are following for another repeat. Opposite Last Decision is the second most often used method, and is used to play alternating win patterns. It is used exclusively for playing alternating single win patterns. They are common for short spurts, but usually not for patterns of five or more repeats.

There are many kinds of repeating patterns, and all, except single alternating win patterns, are played using a combination of *Same as Last Decision* and *Opposite Last Decision* Bet Selection Methods, depending on the pattern of decisions being followed for a repeat.

Figure 11 in Chapter 12 shows a scorecard with a long alternating single win pattern that would be bet using this method. I won 14 hands in a row beginning with PLAYER hand number 8. This was a significant win, and quite simple when you follow the current trend. Good players know that Baccarat is a game of streaks and patterns that provide many excellent opportunities. Good Baccarat players win, and win consistently, by going with the flow!

3. Bunched TIE Repeats

TIE's have a tendency to occur in bunches, particularly in TIE-RICH Shoes. These TIE patterns have only a few decisions between multiple TIE outcomes. Chapter 12 presented the statistical basis for this method, and highlighted the principle indicators used to determine if there may be a good opportunity. If so, bet TIE for each of the next four to six decisions looking for a repeat TIE.

Review the scorecard in Figure 13. Notice the bunched TIE's beginning with the TIE after BANK win number 4. I won eleven of the 15 TIE's, in the Shoe. The best way to play this pattern is to wait for the first TIE decision, then see if another TIE occurs within the next seven decisions. If another TIE does occur, this is the signal to bet TIE for the next four to six decisions. Use relatively small wagers for the TIE bets, along with a bet on the PLAYER or BANK, depending of course on the current pattern of outcomes for PLAYER and BANK.

Rarely do I bet just the TIE by itself. Basically, two bets are working for the next four to six decisions. If there is another TIE, increase the bet, and continue to bet TIE for another four to six decisions.

4. Pattern TIE Repeats

Pattern TIE repeats are repeat TIE's that have roughly the same number of decisions between them. For example, refer to Figure 16 in Chapter 12. Each of the TIE decisions occurred within 12 to 13 decisions of one another. Watch for this kind of TIE repeat pattern, and bet on it to continue. Sometimes TIE decisions are not bunched, but there is a repetitive pattern to them.

Along with pattern TIE repeats, are repeats of the decisions following TIE's. Refer to Figure 10 in Chapter 12. The decision pattern after TIE-4 is nearly a perfect match with the decisions following TIE-6. Study the outcomes of the decisions following TIE's, and consider repeat patterns.

5. TIE After TIE

Bet TIE to repeat immediately after a TIE decision. These are consecutive TIE's. When a TIE decision occurs, bet TIE to repeat on the next decision. I recently won one sequence of five consecutive TIE's, the most I have ever seen playing Baccarat.

In the statistics presented in Chapter 12, there were over 300 occurrences of consecutive TIE's, this includes doubles, triples and more. Refer to Figures 13, 14 and 15 for excellent examples of why I routinely use this Bet Selection Method.

If the TIE decisions are not Bunched TIE Repeats, make only one wager on TIE after a TIE. On the other hand, if the Shoe has been very good for bunched TIE outcomes, continue to bet TIE according to Bet Selection Method 3 for bunched TIE's.

TIE wagers are always second bets. That is, a bet on the PLAYER or BANK (selected using a separate Bet Selection Method) is made right along with a bet on TIE.

6. First and Last TIE's

I have found it profitable to bet TIE on the first and last decision of every Shoe, particularly when TIE opportunities in previous Shoes have been good. However, I suggest picking your spots, rather than making it a routine bet.

If you do make it a routine bet like I do, bet the minimum amount on TIE for the first decision, and for the last decision, make a bet based on the TIE results of the Shoe. The last hand of the Shoe will be announced before the deal of the final hand to give players the opportunity to reconsider their final wagers. Typically on the last decision of the Shoe, my TIE wager will be quite a bit larger than the first-hand TIE bet, and substantially larger if the Shoe has been TIE-RICH.

7. Early and Late TIE's

In addition to first and last decision TIE bets I also make early and late TIE wagers. These are TIE wagers on the first and last four to six hands of the Shoe. Normally I make a small TIE bet on the first four hands of the Shoe. This is a routine wager when previous Shoes played during the same session have had good TIE opportunities.

Late TIE's can also be good bets depending on the overall results of the Shoe up to the last few decisions. For TIE-RICH Shoes, I routinely bet TIE on the last four to six hands of the Shoe. These bets will also be significantly larger than early TIE bets, particularly for TIE-RICH Shoes.

However, it is sometimes difficult to determine how many hands are left to play in the Shoe. If you are keeping a scorecard it will be fairly easy to determine the total number of hands played, ask the dealer, or look at the top of the Shoe for the yellow marker. The last hand of the Shoe is always announced and is indicated by the appearance of the yellow marker that was placed at the back of the eight decks of cards during the shuffle.

8. No Bet

What Bet Selection Methods should be applied to those tough-to-play outcomes, which I call Random Decision Outcomes, or RDO's? Recall that RDO's favor the Casino so overall play must be defensive in nature. Thus, the amount of any bets made must be relatively small, and often, only for the table minimum.

The next five Bet Selection Methods are used to play RDO's. One method is negative and four are essentially neutral. The negative method is *No Bet*. It is used to stop continuing losses. The *No Bet* Method is simply that, stop betting and either sit-out a few hands, or quit and play again later. If you decide to sit-out a few hands, tell the Dealer no bet and wait for a good opportunity. This is acceptable, and a normal part of the game. Unlike Blackjack, you do not have to make a bet on every decision.

In Baccarat, skip a few hands when losing, and better yet, do not make another bet until a favorable opportunity is presented. This is a very important advantage. From my observations, very few Baccarat players make the best use of it. Continue to keep score and watch carefully for an opportunity. I have played entire games while making only a few bets, but winning most of them.

When you are the only player at the table, you can continue to play for several hands while not making bet. Just ask the Dealer to deal a few hands, often they will be happy to accommodate you.

When in doubt, don't bet. Conserve your bankroll for those opportunities that provide the best possible advantage. For less experienced Baccarat players, this is the preferred method for any RDO sequences. It should also be the first choice when one is losing more decisions than one is winning. At such times it is best to simply quit and conserve ones bankroll for another session. When a player is not getting decent opportunities, or is off his or her game, why fight it?

Quit and wait for a better opportunity that will surely come along later. Never chase losses in Baccarat! Often the decision to stop betting will make the difference between a winning and losing session; I use it often.

9. Opposite The Decision Before TIE

After a TIE, bet the opposite of the decision that occurred before the TIE. I do this consistently with two exceptions: when there is a consecutive winning streak in progress, and when the outcomes of previous decisions after TIE's indicate a dominate pattern.

When there is a winning streak underway, the TIE decision merely interrupts the streak, and I will always bet the same as the decision before the TIE. I am therefore betting that the winning streak will continue. Recall the definition of a winning streak is three or more consecutive wins.

As an example to address the other exception, if after nearly every TIE, BANK wins the next decision, I will bet BANK after a TIE. The dominate winner after TIE decisions was BANK. Otherwise, I will always bet the opposite of the decision that occurred before the TIE.

I use this method not because I have statistics to support it, but because I want my play to be consistent. I do not want to be wasting time second-guessing myself. I could just as easily decided to bet the same as the decision before a TIE. My preference is simply to always bet the opposite of the decision before TIE.

10. Follow Table Winner/Opposite Table Loser

Follow the player that cannot seem to lose; or bet the opposite of the player who can't seem to win. If you play RDO's, perhaps the best method to use is *Follow Table Winner/Opposite Table Loser*. Take the recent case of the Mini-Baccarat player whom, after buying-in for only $600, left the Gold Coast Casino in Las Vegas with some $400,000. This is particularly amazing based on his small starting bankroll. After winning a fairly sizable sum he was consistently betting the table maximum of $5,000 per hand, and continued to win! He played 22 hours straight.

The story goes that he was playing at a full table, and his fellow players apparently did not jump-on the winning bandwagon with him. If they had, the Casino would have lost a fortune! Well, that is exactly what his fellow players should have done! In this case, *Follow Table Winner*, was the method the other players at the table should have used to select their bets. That is, let the winner make his bet and bet the same way. In Basketball the hot-hand gets the ball. In Baccarat, bet the same as the big winner.

At other times, the opposite scenario works just as well, if not better. Simply determine who is the big loser, wait for him to bet and bet the opposite. Most times it is very easy to spot the table loser; just listen to his complaints. And yes, they are usually men.

This method is very good for RDO's, but you can also use it at any time. Playing smart means going with the flow and using all the means at your disposal to win, including the use of another player's fortunes as well as their misfortunes! On the many occasions when I am *In-the-Zone* it seems as though I cannot lose. During such times, I sometimes notice that all players at the table are waiting for me to place my bet, before making their own wagers, the same as mine! I don't mind at all, everyone wins!

11. Dominance

Bet on the current dominating winner of the Shoe. This is easily determined since the number of cumulative wins for BANK, PLAYER and TIE's are being scored separately. Dominance is when one side has won at least 15 more decisions, or a fairly high percentage of the decisions (20% or more).

If the dominance continues and you bet on the dominant side, you will win more hands than you lose. However, this will not guarantee an overall win. If your losing bets are consistently higher than your winning bets, you may be an overall loser even though more hands were won.

The dominance method is best applied as an additional check in the Bet Selection process. If no other trend or pattern is apparent, or there is some doubt about what bet to make in a dominant Shoe, bet what has been dominating, or do not bet.

12. Follow BANK / Follow PLAYER

Because some players are partial to BANK or PLAYER, simply bet on BANK following each BANK win, or bet PLAYER following each PLAYER win. Do not make a bet until the side you are following wins. Then continue to bet that side until you lose the bet.

Obviously for this method to be profitable, there must be at least two consecutive wins by either BANK or PLAYER.

I do not use this method by itself. Instead, I find it useful as a check and balance against other methods that may be a better first choice.

Summary

These are the twelve basic Bet Selection Methods - what to bet on and when. How much to bet is the subject of the next Chapter, Money Management Systems.

"Without a plan for completion, it just won't happen."
Robert Half

17 - Money Management Systems

One of the most often written about subjects is Money Management. Of course it has an application to any Casino game one chooses to play. But, it is also the subject that is the most misunderstood.

To be successful at any Casino game requires a basic plan of attack. As a player you can choose what games to play, what bets to make and when to make them, how much to bet, and when to quit. With a plan, these decisions are pre-determined; they are made in advance of any gambling session. When circumstances call for a decision to be made, a properly prepared plan will make the decisions automatic. Your plan has considered all the possible scenarios, and the corresponding decisions that must be made to respond to them, in advance. The traditional themes of Money Management should be a part of this overall plan, but not in the traditional sense. Its meaning is far too broad. That is why the word **Systems** is added. Its use in this context has a much narrower focus, and therefore, a more meaningful purpose.

The subject of Money Management has a bad rap, even among gaming Authors. One Author describes Money Management as silly, precisely because he has taken the traditional viewpoint; it is everything about managing your gaming money.

The same Author goes on to say that Money Management is junk. Such statements are certainly attention-geters, but in the absence of any logical alternatives or useful perspectives, they are just headlines.

So, just what is Money Management? In and of itself, the subject of Money Management is meaningless when it is not made a part of an overall strategy. Money Management couldn't be simpler from my point of view: it is only about how much to bet!

Bet Selection Methods are used to determine what bets to make and when to make them. Money Management Systems are the bet progressions used to determine how much to bet, in the context of your bankroll and style of play.

Money Management may be generally misunderstood, but when applied to the process of deciding how much to bet, there is no confusion.

> *"If you don't get what you want, it is a sign either that you did not seriously want it, or that you tried to bargain over the price."*
> *Rudyard Kipling*

Bet Progressions: Your Offense

When winning, increase the size of each bet in a manner that will provide a decent return when the winning streak is over. When losing, hold losses to the absolute minimum. Money Management Systems are the individual Bet Progressions used to make successive wagers for a given number of decisions. A Bet Progression is a series of wagers that incorporate an increase or decrease in the amount of each successive bet.

To take full advantage of a good opportunity, consecutive winning wagers must reflect an aggressive increase, while at the same time, preserve a portion of the profit from each winning bet. When you have the best of it, pour on the offensive power!

A good Bet Progression will provide a strong punch, but will also prevent you from going broke. That is, don't play CHEAP when winning, but don't bet the farm either.

How often have you seen a player win bet after bet, wagering the same amount each and every time? Making the same bet over and over again, when one is on a winning streak is not conservative play, its plain stupid play! This would be like a Poker player having a full-house, or four-of-kind, and never raising. The profit given-up on such winning hands would be quite substantial. Some of the opportunities you will get playing Baccarat are often as good as four-of-kind in poker, opportunities that must be exploited.

Of course one can be too aggressive, putting all winnings back into the next bet, again and again. This is just as bad as the card player who never raises with a great poker hand. The key is to reach a middle ground between raising bets too much and giving away the profit, and not raising them enough, thereby giving-up too much of a golden opportunity. A good Bet Progression puts you in that middle ground.

There are three types of Bet Progressions: Up-As-You-Win, Up-As-You-Lose, and Up-For-TIE's. In total, they comprise your playbook; the individual plays that you call in your battle against the Casino.

Bet Progressions provide a pre-determined method of sizing individual bets for a small series of successive wagers. It is an automatic method of increasing the size each winning wager. They are designed to maximize profits, and at the same time, prevent any single loss from wiping-out past profits. Money Management Systems are profit generators, and to some extent, profit savers.

The frequent streaks and patterns in the decisions will provide the skilled player with many advantages. That means increasing the size of each successive bet after every win. This increase must be aggressive, but not so much that any single loss wipes-out all previous profits. A portion of the profit is saved from each win, and the balance is used to escalate the size of each succeeding bet.

How much profit is taken-down from each win depends on your individual betting style. Conservative bet progressions will take down nearly all the profit. Aggressive bet progressions will take down less profit in favor of larger bet increases. Ultimately, at least some profit must be secured after one, or two straight wins.

Generally, aggressive wagering on any favorable opportunity must be employed, but in a manner that is controlled. The use of specific pre-planned Bet Progressions provides this control.

All Bet Progressions are expressed in units. Each unit is designated a specific dollar value, and this value can be modified as required. In this manner one can choose a Bet Progression, and the bets are automatically sized without having to think about it.

For example, a three-bet Bet Progression (often referred to as a series) is expressed: 2-1-2. If the unit value is designated to be $5, the series is: $10-$5-$10. As you win, the size of each unit can be increased. A $10 per unit series would make the same three-bet series $20-$10-$20. Once an individual Bet Progression is selected, play to win each bet in the series.

Using the example three-bet series, if the first bet wins, make the second bet, and then the third bet only if the second bet wins. If any bet in the series is lost, the series ends. Go back to the first bet of the series and start over (perhaps with a lower unit value), or choose a different Bet Progression. When all three bets win, start over with the same series, or increase the unit value of the same series (from $10 to $15 per unit), or select a different series. The variations are limitless.

Devise your own Bet Progressions according to your personal style of play. Keep them short, no more than three successive bets in length. Keeping it simple will make it easier to concentrate on the flow of the game, and the more important Bet Selection process. The progressions I use are only two to three successive bets in length.

Use Bet Progressions that provide an early opportunity to make a profit perhaps even after the first win. A win followed by a loss, or two wins followed by a loss, can still provide a profit.

To summarize:
1. Memorize a few basic Bet Progressions for each category (the three types are: Up-As-You Win, Up-As-You-Lose, and Up-For-TIE's).
2. Keep the number of bets in each progression short; only two to three bets in length.
3. When a specific progression is put into play, stop the progression when any bet in the series is lost.
4. Increase the unit value when winning; be aggressive.
5. Reduce the unit value when losing; make minimum bets, or do not bet at all.
6. Use progressions that provide a profit even when the second or last bet in the progression is lost.

Most wagering activity will be associated with the use of bet progressions for consecutive winning wagers. However, there are times when bets are made to recoup losses, the Up-As-You-Lose Bet Progressions. There are specific situations when this type of progression is appropriate. Unfortunately, they always involve significantly more risk.

A good Money Management System, or Bet Progression, will take into account six important factors:
1. Bet Escalation
2. Profit Taking
3. Measured Risk
4. Stop and Skip Points
5. Quit Points
6. Variation Procedures

Bet Escalation

A series of winning wagers, and for some systems, losing wagers, must incorporate a planned increase in the amount of each successive bet. This progressive increase, in the size of each bet, is bet escalation.

The degree of each successive increase will vary based on individual betting styles; conservative to aggressive, or somewhere in between; the level of risk one is willing to accept; and the current level of ones profit or loss.

Profit Taking

A Bet Progression must include provisions for taking-down some portion of the profit as wins occur. The sooner some profit is secured, the sooner your first win goal is achieved. The amount of profit taken-down will vary among progressions. Conservative progressions will take down nearly all the profit. Aggressive progressions will take down less profit in favor of larger bet increases.

To provide a profit after the very first win, use a Bet Progression with a first wager larger than the table minimum, or your normal minimum bet, whichever is greater. The next (second) bet in the progression will be smaller. The advantage is that after a first bet win, and a second bet loss, a profit is made from the two bets; win one hand, lose one hand, and still make a profit. The obvious disadvantage is the potential loss of the larger bet on the first wager.

Measured Risk

The bet progressions employed will reflect
your personal playing style, with each progression having a unique degree of risk. Determine the level of risk that is comfortable, and weight it against the possible return as opportunities develop. The use of
one type of bet progression, over other alternative progressions, must be a carefully
calculated decision.

Consider the football coach who must decide
what play to call in a given situation. All
choices have various degrees of risk. He
considers his options, evaluates the risk,
and implements his decision knowing the risk
he is willing to accept in a given situation.

Stop and Skip Points

Stop and Skip Points are put into effect
when a pre-determined number of decisions
are lost in succession; betting is stopped
and several hands are skipped before resuming play.

Quit Points

A Quit Point is a pre-determined time when
betting is stopped to avoid continuing
losses. This is most often associated with a
bet progression used to recoup consecutive
losses, the Up-As-You-Lose progressions.

It is also the point in a given game where
the maximum allowable loss limit is reached,
or when a pre-determined number of hands are
lost in succession; quit playing.

Pre-determined quit points must be used for Up-As-You-Lose Bet Progressions, and must be part of an overall playing strategy.

Variation Procedures

Variation Procedures are the techniques employed to modify, or switch from one Bet Progression to another. These procedures will be covered in more detail later. Modifications include upgrades and downgrades, expansions and interchanges.

Recommended Bet Progressions

Think of all of the following bet progressions as football plays in a playbook. As opportunities and circumstances dictate, they can be called and put into action. The ability to read the action, review the playbook, and make the right call at the right time is important. Perfecting this operation requires that one have a playbook containing all of the bet progressions that can be put into play as conditions warrant.

1. Up-As-You-Win Bet Progressions

Up-As-You-Win Bet Progressions provide the ammunition to defeat the Casino when the player has one of those frequent advantages. They are offensive weapons, the plays that put points on the board, sometimes in a very big way.

In a typical Baccarat gambling session there will be many excellent opportunities to rapidly increase the size of ones bets. These increases are made possible by a series of consecutive wins.

A portion of the profit from each bet is put into the next bet, and each successive bet, in an effort to reach higher profit levels.

This is not easy; it requires judgment and practice. Based upon the current trend and profit (or loss), trade-offs must be evaluated. You must decide how much profit should be drawn-down, as opposed to how fast to escalate each bet. A rapid bet escalation may eventually wipeout much of the profit. An escalation that is too slow may, however, unnecessarily limit return, thereby largely missing an important profit opportunity.

Ultimately, the decision to use a rapid (aggressive) bet escalation, a slow one (conservative), or somewhere in-between, must be based on the current outcome of the decisions, and the players won or loss status.

If you have been losing, this may be the best opportunity to win back losses, and make a nice profit as well. You may therefore decide to aggressively escalate each bet after each successive win.

Alternately, if you have been winning, it may also be more appropriate to aggressively escalate each bet, keeping past profits intact, but using the new winnings to pyramid profits.

This is the thought process that must be employed when deciding what bet progression to use, and for what unit value. Therefore, a players bet progression play-book is a very important tool. A few basic progressions, each designed to fit a different set of circumstances, are required.

The football team memorizes its basic formations and individual plays, devoting many hours of practice perfecting them. The same applies to gambling. A systems playbook must be formulated, memorized, practiced and perfected.

The following Up-As-You-Win Bet Progressions offer a good mix of options; from conservative to aggressive. Once the basic progressions are memorized, and thoroughly practiced, it will be easy to modify and switch them as conditions warrant.

Again, use short and simple bet progressions. The betting units can be designated any dollar value, and can be changed at any time.

Up-As-You-Win Doubles

Doubles are designed for two consecutive win attempts. The current decision pattern may show frequent BANK or PLAYER wins of two each or more, or an alternating pattern of single wins; use a double following the pattern.

Conservative Doubles:

Bet #	Units Bet	Cumulative Units
1	1	1
2	2	3

Bet #	Units Bet	Cumulative Units
1	2	2
2	1	3

Medium Doubles:

Bet #	Units Bet	Cumulative Units
1	1	1
2	3	4

Bet #	Units Bet	Cumulative Units
1	2	2
2	3	5

Aggressive Doubles:

Bet #	Units Bet	Cumulative Units
1	4	4
2	2	6

Bet #	Units Bet	Cumulative Units
1	3	3
2	5	8

If the first conservative double is successful, it can be repeated, or the medium double can be used. Again if successful, a medium double can be repeated, or stepped-up to one of the aggressive doubles.

A BANK winning streak of six in a row can be bet using only doubles; there would be three successful doubles.

The second conservative double and the first aggressive double, provide a guaranteed profit if the first bet wins. The second bet, if lost, still provides a profit for the two hands played.

For the first conservative double, both medium doubles, and the second aggressive double, both bets must win to make a profit.

With any double bet progression, never make
the second bet unless the first bet wins.
Start again, or switch to a new progression
after a first-bet loss.

As wins occur, the progressions can be modified. For example, using the conservative
double 2-1; simply change the unit value
from say $5 to $10. The initial winning series of $10-$5 becomes $20-$10. If two conservative doubles are successful at $10-$5,
increase the unit value making the series
$20-$10, then go to the 1-3 medium double at
$10-$30.

With another win, the medium double of 1-3
could be upgraded to $15-$45, or another
conservative double of 2-1, $30-$15, could
be used, and so on.

First having memorized the basic progressions, it is a simple task to switch progressions, or either upgrade or downgrade
the size of one's wagers simply by adjusting
the unit value up or down.

Up-As-You-Win Triples

Triples are attempts to win three consecutive wagers. The current decision pattern
may be frequent consecutive BANK or PLAYER
win streaks of three or more, or a double
win on one side, followed by a single win on
the other. Any good pattern opportunity can
be bet using these progressions.

Conservative Triples:

Bet #	Units Bet	Cumulative Units
1	1	1
2	2	3
3	1	4

Bet #	Units Bet	Cumulative Units
1	2	2
2	1	3
3	2	5

Medium Triples:

Bet #	Units Bet	Cumulative Units
1	1	1
2	3	4
3	2	6

Bet #	Units Bet	Cumulative Units
1	2	2
2	3	5
3	2	7

Aggressive Triples:

Bet #	Units Bet	Cumulative Units
1	4	4
2	2	6
3	3	9

Bet #	Units Bet	Cumulative Units
1	3	3
2	6	9
3	5	14

Again with each win, progress through the selected series. If the second bet loses, begin the series again, do not go to the third bet.

The second conservative triple, and the first aggressive triple both provide a guaranteed profit after a first bet win. The first conservative triple, both medium triples, and the second aggressive triple provide a profit only after wins on the first two bets. But a third bet loss still provides a profit.

Remember, simply increase or decrease the unit value to change the size of all bets in a series. For example, the second conservative triple at $5 per unit is $10-$5-$10; at $15 per unit the same triple is $30-$15-$30.

2. Up-As-You-Lose Bet Progressions

Up-As-You-Lose Bet Progressions are defensive or catch-up systems. They are associated with the recouping of a prior lost bet(s). After a loss or losses, a player may attempt to recover by increasing his wagers. Unless a quit point is used, the player's entire bankroll could be placed in jeopardy.

These systems do have a place in your repertoire, but only when they are used in a prudent and intelligent manner. The use of these progressions will typically follow the unsuccessful use of an Up-As-You-Win progression.

In its simplest form, after a loss double the bet. This is a very dangerous way to play if used improperly.

My method is to use one or more recouping bets instead of the standard doubling-up bet. The recoup bet is used to recover previous losses, not considering commissions owed.

Still these progressions can be very costly if carried to the extreme. Therefore, they must be limited in length; limit them to a series of three bets only. My preference is to limit recoup wagers to just two bets. Thus, they will never be used against any long BANK or PLAYER winning streak. The Switch-Stop rule will come into play after the third loss in a row against a BANK or PLAYER win streak. In such cases, the next bet, if made, would be on the streak, not against it. Three successive recoup bets is the upper limit.

For example, following two straight losses with the Medium Double progression of 2-3, the next bet, using an Up-As-You-Lose progression, would be 5 units. A win recoups the loss. Another loss however, makes it a total loss of 10 units. A second recoup bet would then be 10 units, and a third recoup bet, after another loss, would be 20 units. Continuing recoup bet losses are obviously quite expensive.

The timing of any recoup bet must be carefully considered. That is, a recoup bet does *not*, and generally should not, be made immediately after a loss or losses. Stop betting and skip a few hands, and make recoup bets only when a better opportunity comes along.

Because an Up-As-You-Lose bet progression, according to my definition and use, is a re-coup system, individual bet progressions are meaningless. What is important is memorizing the methodology so recoup bets can be prop-erly employed. The size of individual recoup bets depends of course, on the total number of units lost on the previous bet(s).

Variations

In addition to upgrading (or downgrading) the unit value, bet progressions can also be modified by:
1. Expansion: adding additional bets to the bet progression.
2. Interchanging: converting to a new pro-gression while the current one is still in-process, or switching to a new one, but skipping one or more of its bets.

These modifications can produce many varia-tions. This is why I prefer to have only a small number of basic progressions, and each with only a few fixed bets. This provides a starting point from which a multitude of variations can be adopted. It also provides more flexibility. I am not locked into a long and complex betting series.

Utilizing a few basic and short progres-sions, memorized and perfected, combined with simple variation techniques, is both an easier and more productive approach. It is also easier to concentrate on the other parts of the game requiring more attention. Complex bet progressions take far too much attention away from other more important considerations.

Expansions

Expansions are simply the addition of one or more bets to a bet progression in use. I prefer to add two bets at most.

Suppose that wins continue and the outcomes indicate a repeat of the same pattern: for example two BANK wins, followed by two PLAYER wins. A medium triple bet progression is used. After the third win, expand the bet progression by adding a fourth bet.

Suppose a 2-3-2 bet progression is selected, with a unit value of $25, making the bet series $50-$75-$50. After three wins (two BANK wins and one PLAYER) a profit of 7 units, or $175 is secured. Following the pattern, the next bet will be made on PLAYER, and a new series could be used, or the last series could be expanded. Simply add another bet to the series. Another bet of two units (the last bet of the previous series) could be added for the same unit value, or a larger unit value.

Alternatively, you could reason that a total of seven units were won on the last series, and you want to remain aggressive. You decide to bet 4 units at the same unit value, or $100 for the next bet. A win will provide a total profit of 11 units, or $275. You could also continue to add bets, but I generally prefer to start a new bet progression.

Interchanging

Interchanging is converting to a new bet progression while the current one is still in-process, or switching to a new one, but skipping one or more of its bets (typically the first bet). For example, the previous outcomes indicate a pattern of two successive PLAYER wins, immediately followed by three consecutive BANK wins; bet that this pattern will repeat. Next, select a bet progression. However, no bet progression of five bets in length exists. A progression this long is not needed. Choose a progression of two or three bets. If all of the bets in the first progression win, simply select another progression, and continue to follow the pattern.

Continuing with the example, a 3-6-5 series is selected at $5 per unit as the first bet progression. If all three bets win, another series is selected to complete the wagering plan for the five-decision pattern. The three-bet win produces a profit of 14 units.

Next, a two-bet series of 4-2 is selected, and the unit value is increased to $10, making the series $40-$20. If both bets win, a total profit of $130 will be realized for the five successive winning bets.

Alternatively, after the first three-bet win, use the same three-bet series of 3-6-5 upgraded to a $10 unit value. Skip the first bet of the series, and use only the last two bets of 6-5 or $60-$50. This is called an Interchange. Interchanging also works in the other direction.

Suppose a medium triple is won, and the last bet was $80. Next, go to the conservative double 2-1, but call its first bet the last bet of the medium triple just completed.

Then simply scale back to $40 using the second bet of the conservative double (2-1 for an $80-$40 series, skipping the first bet of $80).

Another way of interchanging is switching to a new kind of bet progression after a bet in the current progression is lost. For example, suppose a medium triple of 2-3-2, at $20 per unit, is used. The first two bets of $40 and $60 win, but the third bet of $40 is lost. Switch-over to an Up-As-You-Lose bet progression to recoup the last loss, in this case, another bet of $40. However, if this bet is lost, stop the series. This is a very aggressive approach.

A myriad of options and variations can be used to modify a basic bet progression. Keep in mind however, that some portion of the profit from each win must be drawn-down.

3. Up-For-TIE's

Some of the best player advantages are associated with TIE decisions. An average Baccarat Shoe will contain seven TIE decisions out of the average total of 80 decisions. But, there will also be Shoes that contain many more TIE's; TIE-RICH Shoes contain an average of 11 TIE's. Many times I have played Shoes with as many as fifteen TIE's. With an 8 to 1 pay-off, they provide some of the best possible opportunities a player can get; nearly a sure thing, or at least the closest to one a player will get in any Casino game.

Therefore, TIE bet progressions are important offensive weapons; I call them Up-For-TIE's progressions. They are used to take advantage of the various TIE decision opportunities. Doing so requires a thorough understanding of the kinds of different opportunities associated with TIE's.

Wagering on TIE's must be a standard bet in specific situations. Many of the so-called experts (who are therefore less sophisticated players) advise against making TIE bets. Their conclusions are erroneously based only on the fact that such bets carry a high Casino advantage; over 14%, similar to the Proposition bets in Craps.

However, experience and supporting analysis of thousands of hands of short-duration play shows that there are many excellent TIE opportunities, particularly in TIE-RICH Shoes. These opportunities are: *Bunched TIE's, Repetitive TIE Patterns, Consecutive TIE's*.

There are two ways to take advantage of these opportunities. First, one could bet TIE on every decision of the Shoe. The player will therefore win every TIE decision. Wagering in this fashion, assuming each bet is for the same amount, will result in an overall loss, unless there are at least nine TIE's.

At $5 per TIE-bet for 80 decisions, of which nine are TIE's, $355 would be lost on the non-TIE decisions, and $360 would be won on the nine TIE's. Under this scenario, the more TIE decisions, the more money one can win. Fifteen TIE's will provide a net profit of $275. I do not, however advocate this TIE-bet method. A better and more profitable technique is to bet TIE's selectively.

That is, bet TIE based on the specific outcomes of the decisions as the Shoe is
played-out. Using selective TIE wagering
methods, a player usually will make, at
most, 25 to 35 TIE bets in any Shoe. This
will result in a savings of at least 55 wagers on non-TIE decisions; at $5 each, this
saves $275.

The 25 to 35 TIE-bets, made according to se-
lective wagering methods, will typically
produce a winning TIE-bet percentage of 50%.
Using a $5 TIE-bet, a Shoe containing eight
TIE's will produce a profit of $55; 25 total
TIE-bets at $5 each, with four TIE wins.
This does not take into account the fact
that certain situations will call for larger
TIE-bets; some will be substantially larger
than $5.

Selective TIE wagering means looking for potential TIE patterns, and betting on them.
Using a few basic rules, including the use
of TIE opportunity indicators, ensures that
all potential TIE opportunities get played
automatically, and sometimes with a fairly
large bet.

Recall the TIE data presented in Chapter 12,
and the two TIE opportunity classifications
covered in Chapter 16; *Repeating TIE Patterns* and *Consecutive TIE's*.

Bunched TIE Bet Progressions

One of the best opportunities is Bunched
TIE's. The number of non-TIE outcomes between TIE decisions is often quite small. In
TIE-RICH Shoes, after a TIE there is a 54%
chance that another TIE will occur within

the next five decisions. In normal Shoes,
there is a 25% chance. The Bet Selection
Method for these opportunities is Bunched
TIE Repeats (Method 3 from Chapter 16). When
a pair of TIE decisions occurs with six or
less non-TIE decisions between them, look
for a second bunched TIE opportunity; bet
TIE for the next four to six decisions. The
following bet progressions are employed to
wager on these important opportunities.

Because these progressions consist of only
two bets, simply repeat the progression when
using them for more than two decisions. I
typically repeat them three times for a total of six TIE bets. A more conservative approach would be to use them for just four
decisions; repeat the progression twice.

Conservative Up-For-TIE's Progression: Bunched TIE's:

Bet #	Units Bet	Cumulative Units
1	1	1
2	1	2

Medium Up-For-TIE's Progression: Bunched TIE's:

Bet #	Units Bet	Cumulative Units
1	2	2
2	2	4

Aggressive Up-For-TIE's Progression: Bunched TIE's:

Bet #	Units Bet	Cumulative Units
1	4	4
2	4	8

Use the conservative progression first. Then
following wins, step-up to the medium and
aggressive progressions. As wins continue,
increase the unit value by 50 to 100%.

Pattern TIE Repeat Bet Progressions

Pattern TIE Repeats, Bet Selection Method 4
from Chapter 16, is also a good Tie-bet
situation. It occurs when there is a repeating pattern to the number of non-TIE decisions between TIE's. Refer to Figure 16 in
Chapter 12; there were four TIE's with
nearly the same number of decisions between
them.

Count the number of non-TIE decisions between the first pair of TIE's, and bet that
the next TIE (the third) will have the same,
or nearly the same, number of decisions between them. Use one of the following bet
progressions for wagering on this TIE opportunity.

Conservative Up-For-TIE's Progression: Pattern TIE Repeats:

Bet #	Units Bet	Cumulative Units
1	1	1
2	1	2
3	1	3

Medium Up-For-TIE's Progression: Pattern TIE Repeats:

Bet #	Units Bet	Cumulative Units
1	2	2
2	2	4
3	2	6

A three-bet bet progression is used because the next TIE may not occur with exactly the same number of decisions between them; possibly one more or one less. This provides a little leeway; one bet plus or minus. Thus, if the next TIE outcome is 12 decisions later, or 14 decisions later, instead of the exact number of 13, the bet will still be a winner. Make only three bets; do not repeat this progression.

TIE After TIE Bet Progressions

Always bet TIE after a TIE decision; a single bet only for each occurrence. This is Bet Selection Method 6 from Chapter 16, and it is used to take advantage of the opportunity classification *Consecutive TIE's*.

TIE's often repeat immediately. After a TIE win, increase the unit value on the next Tie-bet by 50 to 100%, looking for a third straight TIE.

For example, after a TIE decision, bet TIE on the next decision, one unit only. If the bet wins, there has now been consecutive TIE's (two TIE's on consecutive decisions). Bet TIE again on the next decision for up to twice the unit value, looking for a third TIE in a row. These are single bets only. Use the following bet progression. With wins, simply increase the unit value.

Up-For-TIE Progression: TIE After TIE

Bet #	Units Bet	Cumulative Units
1	1	1

Consecutive TIE decisions may occur more than once in a single Shoe. Refer to the scorecard in Figure 14, Chapter 12. The first consecutive TIE, a double (TIE-11 and 12), occurred after BANK win 23. I bet $25 on TIE for the decision following TIE-11, and won TIE-12. I then bet $50 on TIE (doubled the bet) for the next decision, but did not win it. Later, after BANK win 26, there was another TIE, TIE-13. Again looking for another consecutive TIE, I bet $50 on TIE for the next decision, and won TIE-14; a nice payoff of $400.

First and Last TIE's Bet Progressions

First and Last TIE's are also single Tie-bets. First-hand of the Shoe Tie-bets are generally smaller than last-hand of the Shoe Tie-bets. Last-hand bets are significantly larger when the Shoe has been very rich in TIE opportunities. Use the single-bet bet progression presented for TIE After TIE, for First and Last TIE bets.

Early and Late TIE's Bet Progressions

Recall these are bets made on the first and last four to six hands of the Shoe. Again, depending on the number of TIE opportunities in the Shoe, Tie-bets on the last few hands of the Shoe are generally larger than those made on the first few hands. Use the conservative and medium Bunched TIE bet progressions for Early and Late TIE bets.

Use one or two repeats for the conservative progression (up to six bets), and one repeat for the medium progression, or a maximum of four bets.

Wagering on Multiple TIE Opportunities

Refer to the scorecard from Chapter 12, Figure 13. Multiple TIE opportunities must be simultaneously addressed as the Shoe is played-out. These include *First and Last Tie's*, *Bunched TIE's*, *TIE After TIE* and *Early and Late TIE's*, along with the Bet Selection Method used to wager on the BANK and PLAYER. A total of five separate wagering methods are used simultaneously. This is a very good reason for establishing some basic rules, and keeping bet progressions short.

The scorecard in Figure 13 will be used to show how these methods work together. Table 7 is a summary of each TIE wager for the first sixteen decisions of this Shoe. Bets were also made on BANK and PLAYER, but for this exercise, only the bets on TIE opportunities will be examined.

For the first hand (H-1) of the Shoe, use the First and Last Tie's Bet Selection Method for a single bet of one unit. BANK won H-1; a loss of one unit.

The next five TIE bets are based on the Early and Late TIE's method (H-2 to H-6). Through H-5 the total loss is five units. But, there is a TIE (T-1) on H-6, and it provides a win of eight units.

On H-7, use the method Bet TIE After TIE, a single bet only. With the previous win, the bet is raised to two units. However, BANK wins H-7, and the total win is reduced to plus one unit.

Because of the early TIE, a TIE opportunity indicator, the Bunched TIE method is used for the next six hands; bet one unit each. H-7 is included as one of the six hands since we are looking for a TIE repeat within seven decisions following T-1. BANK wins H-8 and PLAYER wins H-9. The total cumulative loss is one unit.

The result of H-10 is a TIE, T-2, and a win of eight units, bringing the total win to plus seven units. The TIE After TIE method is used again for H-11. Here a bet of three units is used because the second TIE, T-2, occurred within four decisions of T-1. BANK wins H-11, and the total win is reduced to plus four units. The Bunched TIE's method is continued, and the bet is increased to two units for H-12.

Decision 12 is another TIE, T-3, and a win of 16 units. The total win is increased to plus 20 units. Based on this TIE, TIE After TIE is used again, and the bet is increased to 4 units for H-13. Another TIE decision (T-4) occurs, and a win of 32 units is secured on H-13. The total win is now plus 52 units.

For H-14, again the TIE After TIE bet selection method is used, and the bet is raised to six units. BANK wins H-14. Continue with the Bunched TIE method for the next six hands, including as before the previous hand (T-14), and using the medium bet progression. BANK wins H-15, but there is another TIE, T-5 on H-16, bringing the total win up to 60 units for 16 hands played. On TIE-RICH Shoes, many more TIE bets will be made due to the large number of TIE opportunities. But the positive result is many TIE wins!

Decision By Decision Wagering Summary

Decision #	Units Bet	Reason For The Wager	Result	Cumul. Units
1	1	First / Last Tie's	B	-1
2	1	Early / Late Tie's	B	-2
3	1	Early / Late Tie's	P	-3
4	1	Early / Late Tie's	B	-4
5	1	Early / Late Tie's	B	-5
6	1	Early / Late Tie's	T-1	+3
7	2	Tie After Tie	B	+1
8	1	Bunched Tie's	B	0
9	1	Bunched Tie's	P	-1
10	1	Bunched Tie's	T-2	+7
11	3	Tie After Tie	B	+4
12	2	Bunched Tie's	T-3	+20
13	4	Tie After Tie	T-4	+52
14	6	Tie After Tie	B	+46
15	2	Bunched Tie's	B	+44
16	2	Bunched Tie's	T-5	+60

Table 7

Summary

Money Management Systems are the various Bet Progressions put into play in your battle against the Casino. As more and more wins are recorded, the bets within these bet progressions can be upgraded, downgraded, expanded, or interchanged.

The Bet Progressions, and the techniques to modify them during play, must be memorized, practiced, and perfected.

To quickly adapt to changing trends, be prepared, flexible and alert. Chapter 21 takes
you through a typical Shoe step by step, decision by decision to demonstrate the con-
cepts and processes in action.

Bet Progression Rules and Guidelines

1. When winning, increase the size of each
   successive bet in a manner that will provide a decent profit when the winning
   streak is over.
2. When losing, hold losses to the absolute
   minimum.
3. A Bet Progression is a series of wagers
   that incorporate an increase, or decrease, in the amount of each successive
   bet.
4. There are three basic types of Bet Progressions: Up-As-You-Win (your best offense), Up-As-You-Lose (for recouping
   losses) and Up-For-TIE's (TIE offense). A
   few of each type must be memorized, more
   of the first and third since they represent your best weapons.
5. Keep the number of bets in each progression short, only three bets or less in
   length.
6. Once an individual Bet Progression is selected, play to win each bet in the series. After a series win, modify the progression, and continue to follow the current opportunity pattern.
7. When a specific progression is put into
   play, stop the progression when any bet
   in the series is lost.
8. Increase the unit value when winning (upgrading), and be aggressive.
9. Reduce the unit value when losing (downgrading). Make minimum bets, or do not
   bet at all.

10.Use progressions that provide a profit
even when the second, or last bet in the
progression is lost.
11.Stop and Skip Points: when a pre-
determined number of hands in succession
are lost, stop betting and skip several
hands before resuming play.
12.Quit Point: pre-determined time when betting is stopped to avoid continuing
losses. Pre-determined quit points must
be used for Up-As-You-Lose Bet Progressions.
13.Modify Bet progressions by Expansion:
adding additional bets to the basic progression. Limit the expansion to two additional bets.
14.Modify Bet progressions by Interchanging:
converting to a new system while the current progression is still in-process, or
switching to a new system, but skipping
one or more of its bets.
15.Up-As-You-Lose Bet Progressions are for
recouping a prior lost bet(s). Recoup
bets must be limited to, at most, three.
Generally do not use them immediately after a loss or losses. Stop betting and
skip a few hands. Use recoup bet(s) only
when a better opportunity comes along.

Baccarat can be a very profitable game for
the player who is prepared, patient, disciplined and goes into the battle with a plan
that is practice-perfected. Establish your
plan, perfect it and stick to it. The Casino
will have a very tough time beating you.

18 – Play Discipline

The saddest stories you'll here about gambling all involve discipline; specifically the lack of it. The player who achieves a big win, and then gives it right back; or the player who carefully plans-out a detailed strategy, only to abandon it in the heat of the action.

The Big If; If Only I

Hindsight is always 20/20. Foresight is nearly always blind, unless you plan for the big if's

> *"For all sad words of tongue or pen, the saddest are these: it might have been."*
> *John Greenleaf Whittier*

You could say *"If only I quit when I was ahead that $125"*. Or, instead you could say, *"When I win $100, I'll put it in my pocket and play with anything more than that until I lose it"*. The difference is it's too late in the first instance.

By establishing a plan before play, the loser who gave back all $125 in winnings, would have only given back $25, and quit with a $100 win!

You could also say *"If only I quit when I lost $50, I would still have the other $50 I lost after that"*.

Or instead, you could say *"If I lose 50% of my bankroll for this game, I'll quit and try again later"*.

Again, it's too late; the damage is already done. But, by planning for the possibilities before play, and sticking to the plan, you will never have the same kind of losing experience.

Plan for the big if's before play, and you won't be asking yourself the big if's when it's too late!

Discipline

According to Webster, discipline is *orderly or prescribed conduct; a rule or system of rules governing conduct*. In fact, all other things being equal, discipline is perhaps the single most important asset a player can possess.

Discipline is a practice. In Casino gaming, it is the outcome of following a prescribed system of rules that govern ones play. It is how you conduct yourself in the heat of the battle against the Casino. The three keys to disciplined play are:
• Develop a specific set of prescribed rules
• Practice-perfect them before play
• Strictly abide by them in actual play

The rules of conduct must first be prescribed because you must have a game plan to win. The rules of play detail how one plays in many specific situations. They dictate responses to certain outcomes.

The rules tell you when to be aggressive, or when to back-off, when to quit, or when to skip a few bets, and so on.

By establishing specific rules for many specific situations, ones responses become automatic. For a given outcome, there will be a corresponding response. And because there are so many situations that require specific responses, you will likely have a dozen or so prescribed rules. Each rule is designed to respond to a specific situation or outcome.

Of course, ones game plan must be thoroughly practiced. With a dozen, or more prescribed rules, practicing will ensure your responses are quick and decisive.

And finally, once the game plan is practice-perfected, a player must trust it. A well-conceived plan, practiced and perfected, enables a reasonably skilled player to quickly adjust to the flow of the game as circumstances warrant. There will be no second-guessing yourself. Winning requires confidence in ones ability, and trust in a plan.

Play Discipline is a key element of the POWER BACCARAT 2 formula. It lays-out specific rules for Bankroll Management and various play techniques and strategies that a player will employ against the Casino.

Bankroll Management rules provide an overall methodology for controlling your gaming money. They establish prescribed rules for handling losses to prevent a wipeout, and provide the means to ensure that wins are protected and not given back to the Casino.

Gambling takes discipline, and it is tough. It is often hard to stick with the things that need to be done to reach a goal. Hannah More said, *Obstacles are those frightful things you see when you take your eyes off the goal*. That is a great definition of play discipline, keeping your eyes on the goal and strictly following a plan to get you there.

I can seldom remember not winning at some point in a Baccarat session. Unfortunately, I still remember leaving the table a loser on many occasions in the past because I failed to stick with the plan.

Play Discipline is the consistent execution of practice-perfected *plays* according to an established game plan. It is the third element of the Power Baccarat 2 formula.

Disciplined Play

There are four factors which collectively make-up the important category of disciplined play:
1. Bankroll Management
2. Win Goals and Profit-Taking
3. Mind-Set and Personal Disposition
4. Pre-Planned Tactics and Strategies

1. Bankroll Management

In a Casino, the only thing certain is that the house will always get its percentage over the long run. When one gambles, you are betting on an uncertain outcome. With that in mind, would you risk all of your money on one roll of the dice, or one hand of cards? Not unless the outcome was a sure thing, and that is never the case in Casino gaming.

What we really do is risk only a small portion of our money on any given outcome. Essentially, we want to be able to stay in the game long enough to get a favorable opportunity, and then make the best of it.

Managing your bankroll until then requires a disciplined approach. That is, an organized, pre-planned set of rules that guide ones play. Put your trust in a game plan that is well thought-out, prepared in advance, and is first practiced and perfected, before actual Casino play. The plan is your coach making all the important decisions. Simply execute the play that is called.

Traditionally Bankroll Management is included within the subject of Money Management. However, it really belongs within the subject of Play Discipline.

Bankroll

Bankroll is the total amount of money you bring to use against the Casino. It is the money used only to play Baccarat. The objective is to at least double it. Hotel, meals, and other expenses are extra.

The size of a bankroll depends on the total time you will spend playing, and the amount of your minimum bet. The time spent playing must be determined in advance. For example, for a two-night, three-day trip to Las Vegas, first determine the total number "games" you intend to play. That is, how many separate times will you sit down at the Baccarat table and take-on the Casino? I refer to each of these times as Sessions. Each Session could be a partial Shoe, or one or more Shoes.

Next multiply your minimum bet times 50. The result is the minimum amount of money needed for each Session, referred to as the Stake for each Session.

For example, suppose you decide to play ten Sessions during the trip, and your minimum bet is $5. You will need a Stake of $250 for each Session, and a total Bankroll for the trip (ten Sessions) of $2,500. You can also add a reserve in case you decide to play more Sessions. Consider a reserve of two Sessions, or another $500. Therefore your Bankroll for the trip is $3,000.

Bankroll requirements can also be worked out in the reverse. If your Bankroll is limited to $1,000, and your minimum bet is $5, you will be able to play four Sessions. By splitting your Bankroll into pieces, corresponding to the number of Sessions, you have several individual opportunities to take your best shot at the Casino.

Each piece is your Stake for one session. This is the amount of cash you will take with you to the table. In the example, exchange the entire Stake of $250 for chips. Never exchange your Stake piecemeal, you will want the Casino to record your buy-in for rating purposes.

Each Session must also have a Stop-Loss Point (SLP). An SLP is a pre-planned condition; the Casino has won this game and you withdraw taking your losses with a portion of the Session Stake still in tact. This condition is a loss of 50% of the Stake.

For the example, the SLP will be one-half of $250, or $125. If you lose $125, quit. Place the remaining portion of the Stake ($125) back into its Session envelope. Mark the envelope "*Lost $125*".

No single loss will put your entire bankroll in jeopardy. Think of it as a seven-game series, with the winner the one who wins the most points over the seven games. It doesn't matter if you lose an individual game.

In this manner, you will never lose more than 50% of your total Bankroll. In the example, you will not leave with less than $1,500 of the $3,000 Bankroll. But, you must be **willing, and able** to lose 50%, and no more, of your $3,000 Bankroll.

Together with the Session rule, the worst that can happen is a loss of half your Bankroll. If you are not comfortable with this bring less money, and reduce the number of Sessions.

Gamble only with money you can really afford to lose. Playing short, or with scared money is a losing proposition. The objective is winning; that takes a little money, some skill and a game plan.

In addition to an SLP, use a Consecutive Loss Stopper (CLS). A CLS is a pre-planned point when you quit outright. For example, a CLS could be a loss of five consecutive bets. If five bets in a row are lost, end the Session, even if the SLP for the Session has not been reached. Experience has taught me that more losses typically follow, so why fight it.

To summarize, lets look at the final plan for the example Bankroll:

Total Bankroll:	$2,500
Reserve:	$500
Stake per Session:	$250
Total required For 10 Sessions:	$2,500
Stop-Loss Point (SLP) per Session:	$125
Total Bankroll Stop-Loss Point:	$1,500
Consecutive Loss Stopper (CLS):	5 Losses

By following these guidelines for any Bankroll, you will be a more disciplined player, and the downside risk is planned and fixed. The Casino will never break you!

Summary: Bankroll Management

Because financial resources, comfort levels, and styles of play vary, manage your bankroll according to your needs. Most importantly, establish a plan, and stick to it.

As a disciplined player, your Bankroll must be carefully managed; it is your ammunition against the Casino, do not waste it. Utilizing an organized method will help ensure it is controlled. There are many details that must be planned in advance.

You must bring enough money to play, or you will be playing with short or scared-money. Your Bankroll must also be large enough to play as aggressively as your plan allows.

So far we have covered how to determine what your bankroll should be, how it should be divided, and how it should be managed to prevent a wipeout. Now the up-side, when winning, when do you quit?

2. Win Goals and Profit-Taking

Set a realistic initial win goal, plus a series of succeeding wins goals, that you can
traverse like a stepladder. Once the first
win goal is achieved, step-up to the next
one, and so on.

My initial win goal is always to add at least
50% to my Stake per Session. Once I reach or
exceed the initial win goal, I will leave the
table before falling back below it. As I continue to win and pass each succeeding win
goal, I will never allow myself to fall back
below the previous win level achieved.

Continuing with the Bankroll example, win
goals are established as follows:

PLATEAU	WIN GOAL	TOTAL $
1	50%	$125
2	100%	$250
3	150%	$375
4	200%	$500
5	300%	$750
6	400%	$900
Etc.	Etc.	Etc

If I get above the $125 win goal, but still
less than $250, I will leave the table before
going back below $125. This way I am guaran-
teed a win once getting past the initial 50%
win level.

Once you pass any win plateau, never fall below the previous win goal, or the initial
plateau, whichever is greater.

Profit-Taking

The objective is to take-away a profit from each and every Session. Use the following guidelines:
1. Conservative: Quit before falling below the last win goal. Example: you pass $500, quit before falling back below the last win goal of $500.
2. Aggressive: Quit before falling below the previous win goal. Example: you pass $500, quit before falling back below the previous win goal of $375.

Profit Lock-up

Locking-up a profit means to place the money into your Session envelope(s), along with the Stake for that Session. Use the following guidelines:
1. Conservative: Lock-up <u>all</u> profits <u>and</u> the Stake from any profitable Session.
2. Aggressive: Lock up 50% of the profit. Using the profit-balance, add more Sessions, or add it to the Stake of one or more Sessions. With a greater Stake, larger bets can be made.
3. Always lock-up the remaining Stake from any losing session; place it in its applicable Session envelope.

3. Mind-Set and Personal Disposition

Beating the Casino is the objective. But, it's going to take a little effort on your part. Not a lot, but some. You must make the commitment to do what it takes to be a winner.

There are five basic steps that must be taken to provide a decent opportunity to win:

1. Change your mindset, play to win. Fun is a by-product of winning.
2. Get smart, study and learn the game well.
3. Develop a disciplined approach; establish a set of rules that guide play, formulate a game plan and stick to it.
4. Play Hit 'em and Run; know your limits and pick your spots.
5. Practice and perfect the plan before you play in the Casino.

Five relatively easy steps, that's it! They are not mathematical, nor are they loaded with technical information. Common sense, practical knowledge, strict discipline, and practice will no doubt, make a lot of you tough, and maybe even very tough to beat.

Personal disposition is your state of mind and body. Are you confident and relaxed, or are you tired and uptight? Your play will be affected, either positively or negatively, by the way you feel, both mentally and physically.

Athletes must be in top physical and mental condition to perform at their best. For you to perform well, you must also be physically rested, and mentally up for the challenge.

Before and during play, take stock in your physical and mental state. Are you sharp and alert? Is your concentration wavering? When in doubt, take a break to renew and refresh your self.

Finally, playing style; is your basic betting pattern, conservative, aggressive, or somewhere in between? If it is conservative, you will likely not risk very much very often.

But there are times when even the most conservative bettor knows that he must aggressively increase his wagers. When you have an
opportunity, make the most of it.

In other words, be both conservative and aggressive based upon the situation. The degree
of your reaction depends upon your basic betting style. An aggressive player will always
bet more than the conservative player when
the situation calls for a conservative bet,
and more yet when the situation calls for an
aggressive bet. Whether your style is conservative, aggressive, or somewhere in between,
the bottom line is play defensively when losing, and when winning, pour on the offensive
power.

4. Pre-Planned Tactics and Strategies

Formulate a set of rules and guidelines that
are consistently applied throughout play.
Follow them religiously, and without hesitation. At times its tough, but then that's why
they call it discipline.

Teams practice and perfect their game plan
before the big game just as you must. If a
situation calls for a particular play, each
member of the team must execute his assign-
ment, or the play won't be successful.

In Baccarat, if the situation calls for an
aggressive or conservative bet, to take a
break, or simply quit, act according to your
established plan. Do not alter the plan, execute it!

So what will your own playing tactics and strategies be? What set of rules or guidelines will you follow? Considering any plan must be adapted to ones personal needs and style, consider the following guidelines.

Guidelines and Rules for Disciplined Play

"Whatever you do, you need courage. Whatever course you decide upon, there is always someone to tell you are wrong."

Ralph Waldo Emerson

1. Obtain a Bankroll that is large enough to avoid playing with short or scared money.
2. Pre-plan the number of Sessions you intend to play.
3. Determine the required Bankroll; 50 times your minimum bet, times the number of Sessions to be played.
4. Break your Bankroll into equivalent pieces based on the number of sessions to be played. Fully exchange each piece, referred to as Session Stakes, for chips at the start of the Session.
5. Establish a Stop-Loss Point (SLP) for each Session; a loss of 50% of the Session Stake. Quit before, or when the SLP is reached. A 50% SLP for each Session will ensure that no more than 50% of your Bankroll will be lost.
6. Establish a Consecutive Loss Stopper (CLS); a pre-planned point when you quit outright, or stop betting and skip a few decisions. If five straight bets are lost, end the Session, (or at least stop betting) even if the SLP for the Session has not been reached.

7. Establish initial and secondary win goals. Keep track of winnings and losses so you know where you stand at any point during play.
8. Profit Taking: Conservative: Quit before falling below the last win goal. Aggressive: Quit before falling the previous win goal.
9. Profit Lock-up: Conservative: Lock-up all profits and the Stake from any profitable Session. Aggressive: Lock up 50% of the profit; use the balance of the profit to add Sessions, or to increase the Stake of one or more Sessions.
10. Always lock-up the remaining Stake from any losing session.
11. Change Your mindset; prepare well and play to win.
12. Periodically take stock of your physical and mental condition. Quit when tired or when it becomes difficult to maintain a high level of concentration.

19 - Hit'em & Run

A "Hit" is something that is conspicuously successful. The "Run" part is the intention of doing it quickly and doing it decisively. There is no hesitation and no second-guessing. It is the ability to get the most out of any opportunity, and when such opportunities are few and far between, beating a hasty retreat until the next time. Like the song says: " *You gotta know when to hold'em and know when to fold'em*" .

Available opportunities must be aggressively pursued. A player must have a killer instinct when presented with an advantage. When your opponent is on the ropes, there must be no hesitation delivering the knock-out punch!

By the same token, when the Casino has you on the ropes, be defensive. Retreat and protect your Bankroll. Pick your spots, and fight the battle on your terms.

In both of these scenarios, one must use a strictly disciplined approach, and perhaps even more importantly, one must have a certain degree of mental toughness. The degree of ones mental toughness is perhaps the single greatest factor separating the good players from the great players.

The essence of Hit'em & Run, the fourth element of the POWER BACCARAT 2 Formula, is mental toughness. Mental toughness is the ability to concentrate, reason and act successfully under pressure. Mental toughness is like character, something built-up a bit at a time. It produces, more often than not, a successful response, or a HIT!

Mental toughness is also playing to win, as opposed to playing not to lose. When one plays with the primary purpose of not losing, play is defensive in nature. Defensive play is good when it fits the situation, but very bad when circumstances call for aggressive offensive plays, such as any real player advantage.

To be successful, one has to obtain the required knowledge, design and develop a detailed game-plan, practice it to perfect it, learn to recognize player opportunities, and play to win. Playing to win is not easy. It takes mental toughness; first to trust in your ability and execution plan, then to actually have the fortitude to play within it.

Mental toughness has three important prerequisites.
1. Be fully prepared mentally and have a strong sense of self-confidence. You must feel like the basketball player who wants the ball in the final few seconds of a tie game, or relishes the thought of sinking two free-throws for the win with one second on the clock.
2. Be truly willing and able to risk losing a portion of one's bankroll. Mentally, you must not care about losing this money.

3. Gain enough in-the-heat-of-the-action experience. When the pressure is on to perform successfully in any head-to-head competition, including Casino gaming, previous experience is a real advantage.

Armed with the needed self-confidence and experience, and having a certain degree of reckless abandon concerning your money (controlled reckless abandon as my former football coach used to say), will provide at least a minimum level of mental toughness.

Next, the principle issues that comprise mental toughness must be addressed. Issues such as knowing yourself, dealing with negative emotions, the luck issue and so on must be understood and handled.

Hit'em & Run Strategy #1: Know Thyself

All successful players have self-knowledge. They know themselves well enough to know the level of risk they can live with, and have the discipline to stay within their limits. Self-knowledge is one of their most important assets, perhaps even more important than their skill. This self-knowledge is developed over many years of practice, experimentation and actual Casino play.

They have acquired a bankroll sufficient in size to play in the manner that compliments both their game plan and style of play. They are confident and very well prepared.

If ones style is basically fast and loose, it would make little sense to have a conservative game plan. Ones style must compliment the game plan, and at the same time, reflect the size of ones bankroll.

On the other hand, if you have designed a very aggressive game plan, but your style is normally fairly conservative, or your bankroll is a little short, you will find it very difficult to succeed. You will be poorly prepared mentally since all the pieces do not fit together.

Knowing what is comfortable, both in terms of your style and bankroll, enables you to design a game plan that reflects an acceptable level of risk. A plan that fits within your own comfort zone will therefore produce maximum results. Players get in real trouble when they exceed their comfort zone boundaries. I call it playing over the edge.

If your maximum bet is typically less than $10 dollars, one should certainly not play at a $10 minimum table. Playing over the edge brings with it many problems. First, your practice-perfected game plan is now obsolete. Second, you will be playing with a short Bankroll. Third, having to play above your comfort zone, you will be playing on fear. That is, playing not to lose, instead of playing to win. Good players never play over the edge. They know themselves too well to take such silly risks. The bottom line: if you gamble by-the-seat-of-your-pants, that's exactly where you'll end up.

Hit'em & Run Strategy #2: Overcoming Negative Emotions

Mental toughness means having the ability to deal successfully with several negative emotions. These emotions include fear, self-doubt, pride, ego and greed. Fear can be the most difficult to overcome.

Fear

There are two kinds, one is bad and one is good. The first, the fear of losing ones money is the worst kind of fear. It is the hardest fear to overcome, and it will prevent you from ever being successful.

I have known good players with plenty of money, but they just cannot bring themselves to play the way they must to win. The possibility of losing their money is just too hard to deal with. Successful players have no fear of losing their bankroll. They play to win and are prepared to put their money on the line. They have the killer instinct needed when they have the advantage and their opponent is on the ropes.

The average player is really <u>not</u> willing to put their money at risk. Generally the average player plays much too conservatively when the situation calls for aggressive play. The reason they do not play correctly has more to do with the fear of losing than knowing how to play.

In fact, many average players know how to play Baccarat better than many of the big-money players I see at the tables. But, the big-money player has no fear. He or she has the mental toughness needed to be aggressive when game circumstances dictate. Aggressive and bold betting is not stupid unless it is done chasing losses. You must be aggressive when there is a winning opportunity, otherwise in the end, you will likely have lost money.

Conservative play is good, and there is a proper place and time for its use, but when a real opportunity presents itself, aggressive play is absolutely essential. This takes mental toughness; the guts needed in your head to head battle against the Casino.

The average player works hard at a regular job, but when gambling, sees a car or house payment instead of a good bet made at the proper time. Even advanced players may only be average players because they have a propensity for avoiding risk. Either they really can't afford to lose the money, or they haven't developed the required mental toughness (even if they can afford to lose the money). I believe the majority of such player's fall into the former rather than latter category.

Fear of losing will make you a loser every time whether you are an advanced, or even an expert Baccarat player. There are two lessons to be learned: first, gamble only with money you can _really_ afford to lose. Second, develop the mental toughness you need to eliminate, or at least overcome, the fear of losing. You need to address both of these obstacles if you want to win playing Baccarat.

The second kind of fear is the fear of failure. I call it fools fear. It is fools fear because when you do not overcome it you will look very foolish. Most players, particularly the good ones, have at least some degree of fear concerning failure.

This fear is common in most people before any important event. It is that nervous energy and those butterflies in the pit of ones stomach. Whether we are about to deliver a speech, play in a big game, or make a large wager, we have all felt the discomfort of the fear of failure.

How does one overcome this fear? Answer: self-confidence, and that means being very well prepared. To play Baccarat well, one has to have a practice-perfected plan and the discipline and mental toughness needed to execute it in the heat-of-the-action.

Fear of failure can be good because it may be motivational. It requires one to prepare, and to prepare well to be successful. If you had to deliver a very important speech you would likely look very

> *"Fear of Failure; it's a great motivator. Individuals who don't have a fear of failing often seem to fail. It's not so much that they want to be great, they just don't want to be bad. Fear of being bad is a great motivator!"*
>
> *Joe Montana*

foolish if you had not prepared for it, and practiced your delivery several times. The same applies to Baccarat. Show me a player who is well prepared and mentally tough, and I'll show you a winner.

Hit'em & Run Strategy #3: Luck Is For Losers

How often have you heard someone in a Casino say "I just didn't have any luck today" or other such phrase about luck? Forget luck, it's only for losers. Luck has no place in a real player's vocabulary. There are only the laws of probability, which you can either fight or use to your advantage.

What really causes a player to lose? If it isn't bad luck, what is it? It is your biggest enemy: Pride and Ego, Ignorance and

Greed (PIG). When using the Hit'em & Run approach, PIG is easily beaten because play is conducted according to a well thought-out and practice-perfected plan. It will have built in procedures and decision points that take ones emotions out of the process. The plan makes the decisions that need to be made automatic; all possible circumstances and corresponding actions required have been anticipated and accounted for.

Pride and Ego usually surface when losing. Instead of quitting with a portion of your bankroll still in tact, you keep playing, keep chasing, and keep losing.

Greed is also the enemy because it can cause you to give back any winnings you were fortunate enough to have earned. Recently I witnessed a $10 Baccarat player, who started with a $200 bankroll, win nearly one thousand dollars over a 2 hour period. An hour later, he left the table broke! He got the silly notion his $1000 win should instead be several thousand. So, he kept playing and gave it all back to the Casino, plus his $200 bankroll! Smart? Sound familiar? Without a plan for what to do when you are losing, and what to do when you're winning, you're sure to be a loser in the end; the PIG will get you!

Hit'em & Run Strategy #4: Pick Your Spots

The game of Baccarat uses eight decks of regular playing cards. The average Baccarat Shoe will contain 80 hands, including seven ties. Therefore, on average, there are 80 opportunities to make a bet.

But, a very important feature of the game is that players are not required to make a bet on every hand. This is extremely important because you can wait-out those sequences of outcomes that are the most difficult to win; those choppy and random decision outcomes. You can pick your spots, choosing to bet only when favorable opportunities present themselves. Carefully picking your spots is the best way to play Hit'em & Run Baccarat.

Typically there are 20 to 30 very good opportunities (out of the 80 total hands in one Shoe) in an average game of Baccarat. These opportunities are the biggest profit-makers, so

"Most of us would rather believe in the impossible than attempt the real."

Paul Von Ringel

your largest bets must be made on them. But, by keeping your bets at the minimum, or not betting at all, until one of these favorable opportunities comes along, your losses will be, at best zero, or at worst very low. As a result, your bankroll will be considerably larger than it would be otherwise, which allows you to be much more aggressive during any favorable run.

If you do not see any of the typical and more profitable patterns and trends, simply do not bet. Conserve your bankroll and wait for a favorable opportunity. Betting only when the advantage shifts in your favor is the Hit'em & Run way to play POWER BACCARAT 2.

Conclusion

How well you know yourself, and how well you are able to deal with your fears and doubts will, to a great extent, determine your success in any Casino game. Players who are blessed with the required mental toughness will always out-perform players of like ability who lack mental toughness.

As an avid golfer it is easy to recognize those players on the PGA Tour who have the right stuff. The performance of David Duval early in the 1999 season is a good example. He was spectacular, truly the ice-man of the Tour. What set Duval apart from all the rest of the players at this time was his mental toughness. His ability to keep his focus in the face of tremendous pressure was unmatched by any other player.

In gaming, as in golf, one experiences much the same range of emotions; fear, pressure, pride, ego, greed and so on. One overcomes them, or at least controls them, by developing a high degree of self-confidence through proper preparation, practice and actual Casino play.

Additionally, one must play within his or her comfort zone, playing to your strengths and taking advantage of opportunities.

Finally, one must have the character to grasp success and turn adversity into opportunities. Character and mental toughness are the intangibles that very often make-up the difference between just wanting to win and actually winning.

So how can a player develop and improve his or her mental toughness?

1. Become a proficient player; study and practice.
2. Determine how much money you can comfortably put at risk during any one gaming session without playing not to lose. You must play to win.
3. Play at a table that has the proper limits for the amount of money you have to put at risk. If you are comfortable playing for a $5 or $10 minimum bet, you cannot play at a table with a $25 minimum.
4. Develop a plan that fits within your dollars-at-risk comfort zone. Practice and perfect the plan. Include loss and stop limits in the plan.
5. Be aggressive only when you have an opportunity. Increase the size of your bets as you win, not as you lose. Do not chase losses.
6. Wait until a potential opportunity shows, and until then, be conservative or do not bet at all. Be patient; pick your spots.
7. Turn mistakes into opportunities. Make a note of any errors in judgment, negative emotional responses, or deviations from your plan. These are important lessons-learned; understand why such erroneous responses were made, adjust your plan accordingly and do not repeat them.

20 - Putting A Game Plan Together

A Game Plan is an organized, pre-planned and practice-perfected strategy designed to beat the Casino. It has several parts, and within each, individual techniques and strategies that are employed as circumstances warrant. The Plan establishes specific benchmarks to ensure consistent play; the corresponding actions that must be executed in response to specific outcomes. The decisions required to implement these actions are automatic. The Plan has built-in procedures and reaction-points to ensure disciplined play. The following is a summary of these rules and guidelines - the Game Plan:

Part I: The Basics

1. Memorize the automatic card-draw rules to protect your interest. If an error occurs, get a ruling from the Casino Supervisor before the next hand is dealt.

2. Carefully watch the Dealers post commissions, they sometimes make mistakes.

3. Occasionally pay-off or reduce commissions when obtaining change, or when they have become fairly large. It is easier to keep track of the commissions owed for smaller dollar amounts.

4. Keep interruptions of play to a minimum. Frequent commission payments and cash for chips transactions are annoying to the other players, and a nuisance for the Dealer.

5. Keep a scorecard to record each decision, and apply a consistent scoring technique. Keep completed scorecards for later review and analysis.

6. Determine the current pattern or trend before playing in an in-progress game. Do not bet against the trend.

7. Start play with a new Shoe rather than a partial one, unless there is a good opportunity.

Part II – Golden Rules

8. Go With the Flow. Never ever bet against a consecutive winning streak.

9. Switch sides after losses to three consecutive PLAYER or BANK wins, or stop betting - the Switch-Stop (SS) Rule.

Part III - Key Wagering Opportunities

10. Learn the typical streaks, patterns and trends. Bet on them to continue or repeat.

11. Watch for Repetitive TIE pattern opportunities. TIE's often repeat with only a few decisions between them, and in repetitive patterns.

12. Bet TIE after a TIE - consecutive TIE's are common.

13. Bet TIE on the first and last decisions of the Shoe.

14. Consider making early and late TIE bets - the first four and last four decisions of the Shoe.

Part IV - Taking Your Shot At The Casino

15. When winning, increase the size of your bets in a manner that will provide a decent profit when the winning streak is over.

16. When losing, hold losses to the absolute minimum.

17. When in doubt, bet the minimum, or don't bet at all. Skip a few bets and bet only when there is a good opportunity.

18. For consistency, bet PLAYER on the first hand of the Shoe, unless you hold the Shoe, or cut the cards, then bet BANK. At any other time during the game, bet on the trend or pattern. Do not bet BANK simply because you hold the Shoe.

19. A Bet Progression is a series of wagers that incorporate an increase or decrease in the amount of each successive bet. There are three types of Bet Progressions: Up-As-You-Win (your best offense), Up-As-You-Lose (for recouping losses) and Up-For-TIE's (your offense for TIE decisions). Memorize a few of each of the types and practice putting them in play.

20. Keep the number of bets in each progression short, three bets or less in length.

21. Once an individual Bet Progression is selected, play to win each bet in the series. After a series win, continue to follow the current opportunity pattern.

22. When a specific progression is put into play, stop the progression when any bet in the series is lost.

23. Increase the unit value when winning (upgrading); be aggressive.

24. Reduce the unit value when losing (downgrading); make minimum bets, or do not bet.

25. Use progressions that provide a profit even when the second, or last bet in the progression is lost.

26. Modify Bet Progressions by Expansion: adding one, or at most two bets to the basic progression.

27. Modify Bet progressions by Interchanging: converting to a new system while the current progression is still in-process, or switching to a new system, but skipping one or more of its bets.

28. Up-As-You-Lose Bet Progressions are used for recouping a prior lost bet(s). Recoup bets must be limited to, at most, three. Generally do not use them immediately after a loss or losses. Stop betting and skip a few hands. Make recoup bet(s) only when a better opportunity comes along.

29. Up-For-TIE's Bet Progressions are used to take advantage of TIE opportunities. Be aggressive when playing TIE-RICH Shoes.

Part V - Conserving Your Bankroll

30. Stop and Skip Points: after five losses in succession, stop betting and skip several hands before resuming play, or quit. Pre-determined stop points must be used for Up-As-You-Lose Bet Progressions.

31. Quit Point: pre-determined time when betting is stopped to avoid continuing losses.

Part VI - Bankroll Management

32. Obtain a Bankroll that is large enough to avoid playing with scared money.

33. Pre-plan the number of Sessions you intend to play.

34. Determine the required Bankroll; 50 times your minimum bet, times the number of Sessions to be played.

35. Break your Bankroll into equivalent pieces based on the number of Sessions to be played. Fully exchange the cash for each piece, referred to as the Session Stake, for chips at the start of the Session.

36. Establish a Stop-Loss Point (SLP) for each Session; a loss of 50% of the Session Stake. Quit before, or when reaching your loss limit.

37. Set a Consecutive Loss Stopper (CLS); a pre-planned point when you quit outright, or stop betting and skip a few decisions. End the Session if five straight bets are lost.

Part VII - Win Goals and Profit-Taking

38. Establish win goals and keep track of your winnings and losses so you know where you stand at any point during play.

39. Do not give back profits; take a profit. Conservative: Quit before falling below the last win goal. Aggressive: Quit before falling below the previous win goal.

40. Profit Lock-up: Conservative: Lock-up <u>all</u> profits <u>and</u> the Stake from any profitable Session. Aggressive: Lock up 50% of the profit and apply the balance to the Stake of one or more Sessions, or add Sessions.

41. Always lock-up the remaining Stake from any losing session.

Part VIII - Shaping-Up

42. Change your mindset - practice and play to win.

43. Periodically take stock of your physical and mental condition. Quit if tired, or when concentration becomes difficult.

44. Play Hit'em & Run - know yourself, prepare well and develop mental toughness.

45. Become a proficient player; study and practice.

46. Determine how much money you can comfortably put at risk during any one gaming session without playing not to lose. You must play to win.

47. Develop a plan that fits within your dollars-at-risk comfort zone. Practice and perfect the plan. Play at a table that has the proper limits for your bankroll.

48. Be aggressive when you have an opportunity. Increase your bets with wins, not as you lose; do not chase losses, be patient.

49. Wait for potential opportunities, until then, be conservative or do not bet.

50. Turn mistakes into opportunities; understand why you made them, adjust your plan accordingly and do not repeat them.

Summary

There are many details to plan and consider when putting together a comprehensive game-plan. A carefully thought-out and practice-perfected plan will make it very difficult for the Casino to beat you.

> *"When you're afraid, keep your mind on what you have to do. And, if you have thoroughly prepared, you will not be afraid."*
> *Dale Carnegie*

But, no plan will guarantee a win; it will only provide the best possible opportunity to win. A well-conceived plan, that is thoroughly practiced, will provide the confidence needed to give it your best shot - decisive and consistent play, without fear or hesitation.

SECTION IV

PREPARE & PRACTICE

21 - Baccarat Shoe Played-Out

This Chapter contains an actual Shoe played-out decision by decision. Many of the methods, techniques and strategies outlined in this book are illustrated.

This Shoe was played with a Session Stake of $1000. The Win Goals, Profit-Taking and Bankroll Management strategies used are summarized below:

"A failure is a man who blundered, but is not able to cash in on the experience."
Ellert Hubbard

Session Stake:	$1000
Stop-Loss Point:	$500
Win Goals:	50% or $500
	100% or $1000
	200% or $2000
	Etc.
Profit Taking:	Very aggressive; quit before falling below 2nd previous win goal
Consecutive Loss Stopper	Five consecutive decisions

As the Shoe was dealt, I completed a standard format-card for each hand. These cards take you through the Shoe decision by decision, and will help you understand the thinking process I go through as I play.

The cards contain several kinds of notes and a brief narrative of the rationale used to support specific bet(s).

186

Before each hand is dealt, notes regarding
the following subjects will be recorded on
the standard format-cards (one for each
hand):
1. Trend / Pattern
2. Bet Selection Method and Bet Progressions
3. Rationale / Comments

The specific bet(s) made are also recorded,
then the hand is dealt.

Next, the results of the hand were recorded
on the format-card including the actual cards
dealt, the total of the cards, the winner of
the hand, the cumulative score of the Shoe
and the cumulative win or loss in dollars.

A Baccarat practice scorecard was also completed hand by hand as the Shoe was dealt.
This practice scorecard will be introduced in
the next Chapter, and is an excellent practice tool.

At the conclusion of this exercise, a statistical analysis of the results of the Shoe is
presented. This critical evaluation process
is an important tool for improving practical
skills and overall play. Two to four additional wins the next time may be the difference between a winning and losing Session.

To begin the
Shoe, eight
decks of cards
have been shuf-
fled, laced,
and cut. The
first card is
turned over, a
five, requiring

*"You make your first mistake
by playing unprepared. Now
demonstrate courage by
learning and then being
determined to win."*
Harvey Mackay

that five cards be burned and discarded. Play
begins.

Hand Number: 1

Trend / Pattern: NONE

Bet Selection Method: FIRST & LAST TIES, EARLY & LATE TIES

Bet Progression: CONSERVATIVE DOUBLE 2-1, $20/UNIT; CONSERVATIVE BUNCHED TIES $/UNIT

Rationale / Comments: I ALWAYS BET BANK ON THE FIRST HAND WHEN I CUT THE CARDS, OTHERWISE I BET PLAYER. I ALWAYS BET TIE ON FIRST HAND AND LOOK FOR EARLY TIES WITHIN THE FIRST 4 TO 6 DECISIONS — I START CONSERVATIVE AND BET TIE FOR FIRST 4 HANDS

Bet $ BANK: 40	Bet $ PLAYER:			Bet $ TIE: 5	
PLAYER Cards:	3	10	K	Total: 3	
BANK Cards:	5	6	6	Total: 7	
Result:	BANK: ✓		PLAYER:	TIE:	
Cumul. Score:	BANK: 1		PLAYER: 0	TIE: 0	
Cumulative Win / (Loss) $: +35 (WON 40, LOST 5 TIE)					

Hand Number: 2

Trend / Pattern: NONE

Bet Selection Method: SAME AS LAST DECISION; CONSERVATIVE BUNCHED TIES FOR EARLY TIES

Bet Progression: SECOND BET OF DOUBLE, FIRST BET OF CONSERVATIVE BUNCHED TIES

Rationale / Comments: THE FIRST TIE BET WAS ONE UNIT FOR FIRST HAND TIE, THIS STARTS THE BUNCHED TIE BET PROGRESSION I AM LOOKING FOR A TIE WITHIN FIRST 4 DECISIONS.
BANK WON FIRST — I STAY WITH BANK

Bet $ BANK: 20	Bet $ PLAYER:			Bet $ TIE: 5	
PLAYER Cards:	8	2	7	Total: 7	
BANK Cards:	3	4	—	Total: 7	
Result:	BANK:		PLAYER:	TIE: ✓	
Cumul. Score:	BANK: 1		PLAYER: 0	TIE: 1	
Cumulative Win / (Loss) $: +75 (WON 40 ON TIE)					

Hand Number: 3

Trend / Pattern: POTENTIAL TIE PATTERNS

Bet Selection Method: TIE AFTER TIE ; OPPOSITE THE DECISION BEFORE TIE

Bet Progression: TIE AFTER TIE - DOUBLE UP ! CONSERVATIVE DOUBLE 2-1 UPGRADED TO $25/UNIT

Rationale / Comments: DOUBLE TIE BET LOOKING FOR ANOTHER TIE (CONSECUTIVE TIES).

SWITCH TO PLAYER BASED ON STANDARD METHOD OF OPPOSITE THE DECISION BEFORE TIE.

Bet $ BANK:	Bet $ PLAYER: 50		Bet $ TIE: 10
PLAYER Cards:	6	A	—	Total: 7
BANK Cards:	5	K	2	Total: 7
Result:	BANK:	PLAYER:	TIE: ✓
Cumul. Score:	BANK: 1	PLAYER: 0	TIE: 2
Cumulative Win / (Loss) $: +155 (WON $80 ON TIE)			

Hand Number: 4

Trend / Pattern: TIE PATTERNS

Bet Selection Method: TIE AFTER TIE ; OPPOSITE THE DECISION BEFORE TIE

Bet Progression: TIE AFTER TIE - DOUBLE UP ; MEDIUM TRIPLE 1-3-2 AT $25/UNIT

Rationale / Comments: THE TWO TIES ARE A GOOD INDICATOR OF A TIE-RICH SHOE

I INTERCHANGE TO A MEDIUM TRIPLE STARTING WITH SECOND BET

Bet $ BANK:	Bet $ PLAYER: 75		Bet $ TIE: 20
PLAYER Cards:	6	10	—	Total: 6
BANK Cards:	K	J	A	Total: 1
Result:	BANK:	PLAYER: ✓	TIE:
Cumul. Score:	BANK: 1	PLAYER: 1	TIE: 2
Cumulative Win / (Loss) $: +210 (WON 75 LOST 20)			

Hand Number: 5

Trend / Pattern: TIE PATTERNS & REPETITIVE PATTERNS

Bet Selection Method: BUNCHED TIE REPEATS; OPPOSITE LAST DECISION

Bet Progression: MEDIUM BUNCHED TIES - 2 UNITS AT $5 EACH; THIRD BET OF MEDIUM TRIPLE 1-3-2

Rationale / Comments: UPGRADE TIE BET TO STANDARD 2 UNITS

LOOKING FOR A BANK WIN TO CONTINUE THE REPETITIVE PATTERN OF ALTERNATING SINGLES

Bet $ BANK: 50	Bet $ PLAYER:			Bet $ TIE: 10	
PLAYER Cards:	6	9	6	Total:	1
BANK Cards:	5	5	9	Total:	9
Result:	BANK: ✓		PLAYER:		TIE:
Cumul. Score:	BANK: 2		PLAYER: 1		TIE: 2
Cumulative Win / (Loss) $: +250					

Hand Number: 6

Trend / Pattern: TIE PATTERNS & REPETITIVE PATTERN

Bet Selection Method: BUNCHED TIE REPEATS; OPPOSITE LAST DECISION

Bet Progression: MEDIUM BUNCHED TIES; AGGRESSIVE DOUBLE 3-5 AT $25/UNIT

Rationale / Comments: STAYING WITH TIE BASED ON EARLY DOUBLE

A PLAYER WIN CONTINUES THE PATTERN

Bet $ BANK:	Bet $ PLAYER: 75			Bet $ TIE: 10	
PLAYER Cards:	3	J	J	Total:	3
BANK Cards:	K	10	3	Total:	3
Result:	BANK:		PLAYER:		TIE: ✓
Cumul. Score:	BANK: 2		PLAYER: 1		TIE: 3
Cumulative Win / (Loss) $: +330 (WON $80 ON TIE)					

Hand Number: 7

Trend / Pattern: TIE PATTERNS ; REPETITIVE PATTERN

Bet Selection Method: TIE AFTER TIE ; OPPOSITE THE DECISION BEFORE TIE

Bet Progression: TIE AFTER TIE - DOUBLE UP ; SECOND BET OF AGGRESSIVE DOUBLE 3-5

Rationale / Comments: 3 TIES IN FIRST 6 HANDS - LOOKS LIKE A GREAT TIE-RICH SHOE!

STAYING WITH REPETITIVE PATTERN OF ALTERNATING SINGLE WINS.

Bet $ BANK:	Bet $ PLAYER: 125		Bet $ TIE: 20	
PLAYER Cards:	Q	9	—	Total: 9
BANK Cards:	Q	Q	—	Total: 0
Result:	BANK:	PLAYER: ✓	TIE:	
Cumul. Score:	BANK: 2	PLAYER: 2	TIE: 3	
Cumulative Win / (Loss) $: + 435				

Hand Number: 8

Trend / Pattern: TIE PATTERNS ; REPETITIVE PATTERN

Bet Selection Method: BUNCHED TIE REPEATS ; OPPOSITE LAST DECISION

Bet Progression: AGGRESSIVE BUNCHED TIES - 4 UNITS $5 EACH ; AGGRESSIVE DOUBLE 4-2 AT $25/UNIT

Rationale / Comments: MORE AGGRESSIVE ON TIES UP TO STANDARD $20

BETTING BANK TO FOLLOW ALTERNATING PATTERN

Bet $ BANK: 100	Bet $ PLAYER:		Bet $ TIE: 20	
PLAYER Cards:	K	Q	J	Total: 0
BANK Cards:	8	4	4	Total: 6
Result:	BANK: ✓	PLAYER:	TIE:	
Cumul. Score:	BANK: 3	PLAYER: 2	TIE: 3	
Cumulative Win / (Loss) $: + 515				

Hand Number:	9		
Trend / Pattern:	TIE PATTERNS & REPETITIVE PATTERN		
Bet Selection Method:	BUNCHED TIES ; OPPOSITE LAST DECISION		
Bet Progression:	AGGRESSIVE BUNCHED TIE'S UPGRADED; SECOND BET AGGRESSIVE DOUBLE UPGRADED TO $50/un		
Rationale / Comments:	TIES UPGRADED TO $10/UNIT SINCE THERE WERE 2 DECISIONS BETWEEN LAST 2 TIES AND I AM LOOKING FOR A REPEAT		
	A WIN BY PLAYER WILL MAKE IT A SECOND REPEAT OF THE ALTERNATING PATTERN		
Bet $ BANK:	Bet $ PLAYER: 100		Bet $ TIE: 40
PLAYER Cards:	4 2 —		Total: 6
BANK Cards:	6 Q —		Total: 6
Result:	BANK:	PLAYER:	TIE: ✓
Cumul. Score:	BANK: 3	PLAYER: 2	TIE: 4
Cumulative Win / (Loss) $:	+835 (WON $320 ON TIE)		

Hand Number:	10		
Trend / Pattern:	TIE PATTERNS & REPETITIVE PATTERN		
Bet Selection Method:	TIE AFTER TIE ; OPPOSITE THE DECISION BEFORE TIE		
Bet Progression:	TIE AFTER TIE ; MEDIUM DOUBLE 2-3 AT $75/UNIT		
Rationale / Comments:	BECAUSE $40 IS ALREADY A BIG TIE BET, I ONLY ADD $10 TO MAKE IT $50		
	A PLAYER WIN COMPLETES THE SECOND REPEAT OF THE PATTERN		
Bet $ BANK:	Bet $ PLAYER: 150		Bet $ TIE: 50
PLAYER Cards:	A 9 5		Total: 5
BANK Cards:	7 3 8		Total: 8
Result:	BANK: ✓	PLAYER:	TIE:
Cumul. Score:	BANK: 4	PLAYER: 2	TIE: 4
Cumulative Win / (Loss) $:	+635 (LOST BOTH BETS)		

Hand Number: 11

Trend / Pattern: TIE PATTERNS & REPETITIVE PATTERN

Bet Selection Method: BUNCHED TIE REPEATS; OPPOSITE LAST DECISION

Bet Progression: CONSERVATIVE BUNCHED TIES UPGRADED TO $25/UNIT; MEDIUM DOUBLE 2-3 AT $50/UNIT

Rationale / Comments: WITH 4 TIES IN 10 DECISIONS CONTINUE TO BE AGGRESSIVE

REPETITIVE PATTERN SWITCH TO DOUBLES, LOOKING FOR PLAYER TO WIN TWO

Bet $ BANK:	Bet $ PLAYER: 100		Bet $ TIE: 25	
PLAYER Cards:	6	A	-	Total: 7
BANK Cards:	2	5	-	Total: 7
Result:	BANK:	PLAYER:	TIE: ✓	
Cumul. Score:	BANK: 4	PLAYER: 2	TIE: 5	
Cumulative Win / (Loss) $: + 835				

Hand Number: 12

Trend / Pattern: TIE PATTERNS; REPETITIVE PATTERN

Bet Selection Method: TIE AFTER TIE; OPPOSITE THE DECISION BEFORE TIE

Bet Progression: TIE AFTER TIE DOUBLE UP; SECOND BET OF MEDIUM DOUBLE 2-3 AT $50/UNIT

Rationale / Comments: 5 TIES IN 11 HANDS — A TIE-RICH SHOE
STILL LOOKING FOR TWO PLAYER WINS.
I WENT TO THE SECOND BET OF THE DOUBLE DUE TO LARGER TIE BET — I LIKE MY BANK OR PLAYER BETS TO BE LARGER THAN TIE

Bet $ BANK:	Bet $ PLAYER: 150		Bet $ TIE: 50	
PLAYER Cards:	K	A	Q	Total: 1
BANK Cards:	6	4	K	Total: 0
Result:	BANK:	PLAYER: ✓	TIE:	
Cumul. Score:	BANK: 4	PLAYER: 3	TIE: 5	
Cumulative Win / (Loss) $: + 935				

Hand Number: 13				
Trend / Pattern: TIE PATTERNS; REPETITIVE PATTERN				
Bet Selection Method: BUNCHED TIE REPEATS; SAME AS LAST DECISION				
Bet Progression: MEDIUM BUNCHED TIES, 2 UNITS AT $25 EACH; AGGRESSIVE DOUBLE 4-2 AT $50/UNIT				
Rationale / Comments: SINCE THERE WAS ONE DECISION BETWEEN TIE 4 AND 5, THE PATTERN COULD REPEAT SO I STAY LARGE ON TIE				
LOOKING FOR A SECOND PLAYER WIN TO MATCH THE DOUBLE BY BANK				
Bet $ BANK:	Bet $ PLAYER: 200		Bet $ TIE: 50	
PLAYER Cards:	5	A	−	Total: 6
BANK Cards:	2	6	−	Total: 8
Result:	BANK: ✓	PLAYER:	TIE:	
Cumul. Score:	BANK: 5	PLAYER: 3	TIE: 5	
Cumulative Win / (Loss) $: + 685				

Hand Number: 14				
Trend / Pattern: TIE PATTERNS; REPETITIVE PATTERN				
Bet Selection Method: BUNCHED TIE REPEATS; SAME AS LAST DECISION				
Bet Progression: CONSERVATIVE BUNCHED TIES / UNIT AT $25; CONSERVATIVE DOUBLE 2-1 AT $50/UNIT				
Rationale / Comments: SCALE BACK A BIT TO SEE WHAT DEVELOPS WITH TIES AND A POTENTIAL REPETITIVE PATTERN — LOOKING FOR BANK TO WIN A SECOND DOUBLE.				
Bet $ BANK: 100	Bet $ PLAYER:		Bet $ TIE: 25	
PLAYER Cards:	J	6	−	Total: 6
BANK Cards:	6	9	9	Total: 4
Result:	BANK:	PLAYER: ✓	TIE:	
Cumul. Score:	BANK: 5	PLAYER: 4	TIE: 5	
Cumulative Win / (Loss) $: + 560				

Hand Number: *15*

Trend / Pattern: *TIE PATTERNS ; REPETITIVE PATTERN*

Bet Selection Method: *BUNCHED TIE REPEATS ; SAME AS LAST DECISION*

Bet Progression: *SAME CONSERV. BUNCHED TIES ; SAME CONSERVATIVE DOUBLE 2-1 AT $50/UNIT*

Rationale / Comments: *I WILL STAY WITH TIE FOR TWO MORE HANDS.*
THE TEMTATION IS TO TRY TO RECOUP LAST 2 LOSSES - INSTEAD I STAY WITH IT LOOKING FOR A BETTER OPPORTUNITY - LOOKING FOR A DOUBLE ON PLAYER

Bet $ BANK:	Bet $ PLAYER: *100*		Bet $ TIE: *25*	
PLAYER Cards:	*8*	*K*	*—*	Total: *8*
BANK Cards:	*4*	*K*	*—*	Total: *4*
Result:	BANK:	PLAYER: *✓*		TIE:
Cumul. Score:	BANK: *5*	PLAYER: *5*		TIE: *5*
Cumulative Win / (Loss) $: *+ 635*				

Hand Number: *16*

Trend / Pattern: *TIE PATTERNS ; REPETITIVE PATTERN*

Bet Selection Method: *BUNCHED TIE REPEATS ; OPPOSITE LAST DECISION*

Bet Progression: *SAME CONSERV. BUNCHED TIES ; SECOND BET OF THE CONSERVATIVE DOUBLE 2-1*

Rationale / Comments: *LAST TIE BET UNTIL ANOTHER TIE DECISION*

LOOKING FOR A SINGLE BANK WIN TO FOLLOW DOUBLE THEN SINGLE PATTERN

Bet $ BANK: *50*	Bet $ PLAYER:		Bet $ TIE: *25*	
PLAYER Cards:	*6*	*7*	*7*	Total: *0*
BANK Cards:	*5*	*9*	*6*	Total: *0*
Result:	BANK:	PLAYER:		TIE: *✓*
Cumul. Score:	BANK: *5*	PLAYER: *5*		TIE: *6*
Cumulative Win / (Loss) $: *+835*				

Hand Number: 17

Trend / Pattern: TIE PATTERNS; REPETITIVE PATTERN

Bet Selection Method: TIE AFTER TIE; OPPOSITE THE DECISION BEFORE TIE

Bet Progression: TIE AFTER TIE DOUBLE UP; MEDIUM DOUBLE 2-3 AT $75/UNIT

Rationale / Comments: 6 TIES IN 16 DECISIONS — THE LAST TWO TIES HAD 4 DECISIONS BETWEEN THEM — I WILL LOOK FOR A REPEAT

LOOKING FOR A DOUBLE WIN BY BANK TO REPEAT THE PATTERN

Bet $ BANK: 150	Bet $ PLAYER:			Bet $ TIE: 50	
PLAYER Cards:	10	5	5	Total:	0
BANK Cards:	3	8	8	Total:	9
Result:	BANK: ✓		PLAYER:	TIE:	
Cumul. Score:	BANK: 6		PLAYER: 5	TIE: 6	
Cumulative Win / (Loss) $: + 935					

Hand Number: 18

Trend / Pattern: TIE PATTERNS; REPETITIVE PATTERN

Bet Selection Method: BUNCHED TIE REPEATS; SAME AS LAST DECISION

Bet Progression: CONSERV. BUNCHED TIES / UNIT $25 SECOND BET OF MEDIUM DOUBLE 2-3

Rationale / Comments: SCALE BACK TO $25 ON TIE, BUT ON THE FIFTH HAND AFTER TIE-6 I WILL DOUBLE-UP LOOKING FOR A REPEAT TIE

LOOKING FOR A SECOND BANK WIN, THEN SINGLES AND DOUBLE TO REPEAT PATTERN

Bet $ BANK: 225	Bet $ PLAYER:			Bet $ TIE: 25	
PLAYER Cards:	J	2	Q	Total:	2
BANK Cards:	Q	2	7	Total:	9
Result:	BANK: ✓		PLAYER:	TIE:	
Cumul. Score:	BANK: 7		PLAYER: 5	TIE: 6	
Cumulative Win / (Loss) $: + 1135					

Hand Number: 19

Trend / Pattern:	TIE PATTERNS; REPETITIVE PATTERN				
Bet Selection Method:	BUNCHED TIE REPEATS; OPPOSITE LAST DECISION				
Bet Progression:	CONSERV. BUNCHED TIES / AT $25 AGGRESSIVE DOUBLE 3-5 AT $50/UNIT				
Rationale / Comments:	STAY WITH TIE				
	PLAYING FOR A SINGLE ON PLAYER TO FOLLOW THE B-B-P-B-P.P PATTERN				
	ACHIEVED MY FIRST IMPORTANT WIN GOAL $1000				
Bet $ BANK:	Bet $ PLAYER: 150			Bet $ TIE: 25	
PLAYER Cards:	10	K	—	Total:	0
BANK Cards:	8	10	—	Total:	8
Result:	BANK: ✓		PLAYER:	TIE:	
Cumul. Score:	BANK: 8		PLAYER: 5	TIE: 6	
Cumulative Win / (Loss) $: + 960					

Hand Number: 20

Trend / Pattern:	TIE PATTERNS; POTENTIAL BANK WINNING STREAK				
Bet Selection Method:	BUNCHED TIE REPEATS; SAME AS LAST DECISION				
Bet Progression:	CONSERV. BUNCHED TIES / AT $25 SAME AGGRESSIVE DOUBLE - REPEAT FIRST BET				
Rationale / Comments:	AFTER THIS TIE BET, THE NEXT WILL BE DOUBLED TO REPEAT PATTERN				
	3 IN A ROW FOR BANK MEANS CAUTION - I SWITCH LOOKING FOR POSSIBLE WIN STREAK				
Bet $ BANK: 150	Bet $ PLAYER:			Bet $ TIE: 25	
PLAYER Cards:	2	Q	—	Total:	2
BANK Cards:	9	9	—	Total:	8
Result:	BANK: ✓		PLAYER:	TIE:	
Cumul. Score:	BANK: 9		PLAYER: 5	TIE: 6	
Cumulative Win / (Loss) $: + 1085					

Hand Number: 21

Trend / Pattern: TIE PATTERNS; BANK WIN STREAK

Bet Selection Method: PATTERN TIE REPEAT; SAME AS LAST DECISION

Bet Progression: MEDIUM PATTERN TIE REPEAT - 2 units AT $25/unit; SECOND BET OF AGGRESSIVE DOUBLE 3-5

Rationale / Comments: THIS IS THE 5TH DECISION AFTER TIE-6; A TIE ON THIS HAND WILL REPEAT THE PATTERN OF 4 DECISIONS BETWEEN TIES — THUS THE AGGRESSIVE BET.

4 STRAIGHT FOR BANK — STAY WITH THE FLOW!

	Bet $ BANK: 250	Bet $ PLAYER:		Bet $ TIE: 50
PLAYER Cards:	2	2	6	Total: 0
BANK Cards:	J	4	6	Total: 0
Result:	BANK:	PLAYER:		TIE: ✓
Cumul. Score:	BANK: 9	PLAYER: 5		TIE: 7
Cumulative Win / (Loss) $: +1485 (WON 400 ON TIE!)				

Hand Number: 22

Trend / Pattern: TIE PATTERNS; BANK WIN STREAK

Bet Selection Method: TIE AFTER TIE; SAME AS LAST DECISION (BEFORE THE TIE)

Bet Progression: TIE AFTER TIE; AGGRESSIVE TRIPLE 3-6-5 AT $75/unit

Rationale / Comments: A $50 TIE BET IS ENOUGH SO I REPEAT THE BET AND WILL STAY WITH IT FOR 5 MORE DECISIONS — BUT I WILL INCREASE IT ON THE 5TH LOOKING TO REPEAT THE PATTERN. BECAUSE OF THE BANK STREAK I DO NOT BET THE OPPOSITE OF THE DECISION BEFORE TIE.

	Bet $ BANK: 225	Bet $ PLAYER:		Bet $ TIE: 50
PLAYER Cards:	9	4	3	Total: 6
BANK Cards:	Q	J	9	Total: 9
Result:	BANK: ✓	PLAYER:		TIE:
Cumul. Score:	BANK: 10	PLAYER: 5		TIE: 7
Cumulative Win / (Loss) $: +1660				

Hand Number: 23

Trend / Pattern: TIE PATTERNS; BANK WIN STREAK

Bet Selection Method: PATTERN TIE REPEATS; SAME AS LAST DECISION

Bet Progression: SAME MEDIUM PATTERN TIE REPEAT SECOND BET OF AGGRESSIVE TRIPLE 3-6-5

Rationale / Comments: STAY WITH TIE — SHOE IS TIE-RICH!

5 IN A ROW FOR BANK!
O

Bet $ BANK: 450	Bet $ PLAYER:			Bet $ TIE: 50	
PLAYER Cards:	10	7	—	Total:	7
BANK Cards:	J	8	—	Total:	8
Result:	BANK: ✓		PLAYER:	TIE:	
Cumul. Score:	BANK: 11		PLAYER: 5	TIE: 7	
Cumulative Win / (Loss) $: + 2060					

Hand Number: 24

Trend / Pattern: TIE PATTERNS; BANK WIN STREAK

Bet Selection Method: PATTERN TIE REPEATS; SAME AS LAST DECISION

Bet Progression: SAME AS LAST HAND — THIRD BET OF THE TRIPLE

Rationale / Comments: 3 more TIE BETS

STAY ON BANK UNTIL PLAYER WINS — 6 STRAIGHT SO FAR

PASSED ANOTHER WIN GOAL!

Bet $ BANK: 375	Bet $ PLAYER:			Bet $ TIE: 50	
PLAYER Cards:	2	4	—	Total:	6
BANK Cards:	6	A	—	Total:	7
Result:	BANK: ✓		PLAYER:	TIE:	
Cumul. Score:	BANK: 12		PLAYER: 5	TIE: 7	
Cumulative Win / (Loss) $: + 2385					

Hand Number: 25					
Trend / Pattern: TIE PATTERNS ; BANK WIN STREAK					
Bet Selection Method: PATTERN TIE REPEATS ; SAME AS LAST DECISION					
Bet Progression: MEDIUM PATTERN TIE REPEATS ; AGGRESSIVE DOUBLE 4-2 AT $100/UNIT					
Rationale / Comments:					
2 MORE TIE BETS					
7 IN A ROW FOR BANK — STAY ON IT					
Bet $ BANK: 400	Bet $ PLAYER:			Bet $ TIE: 50	
PLAYER Cards:	A	4	5	Total:	0
BANK Cards:	7	7	3	Total:	7
Result:	BANK: ✓		PLAYER:	TIE:	
Cumul. Score:	BANK: 13		PLAYER: 5	TIE: 7	
Cumulative Win / (Loss) $: +2735					

Hand Number: 26					
Trend / Pattern: TIE PATTERNS ; BANK WIN STREAK					
Bet Selection Method: PATTERN TIE REPEATS ; SAME AS LAST DECISION					
Bet Progression: MEDIUM PATTERN TIE REPEATS - UPGRADE TO $50/UNIT ; SECOND BET OF AGGRESSIVE DOUBLE					
Rationale / Comments: THERE WERE 4 DECISIONS BETWEEN TIES 5 AND 6, AND 6 AND 7 - I AM LOOKING FOR A REPEAT OF THE SAME SO I DOUBLE-UP THE BET.					
8 IN A ROW FOR BANK — STAY ON BANK					
Bet $ BANK: 200	Bet $ PLAYER:			Bet $ TIE: 100	
PLAYER Cards:	10	4	8	Total:	2
BANK Cards:	7	3	2	Total:	2
Result:	BANK:		PLAYER:	TIE: ✓	
Cumul. Score:	BANK: 13		PLAYER: 5	TIE: 8	
Cumulative Win / (Loss) $: +3535					

Hand Number: 27

Trend / Pattern: TIE PATTERNS ; BANK WIN STREAK

Bet Selection Method: TIE AFTER TIE ; SAME AS LAST DECISION (BEFORE TIE)

Bet Progression: TIE AFTER TIE DOUBLE UP ; AGGRESSIVE TRIPLE 3-6-5 AT $150/UNIT

Rationale / Comments: GREAT TIE-RICH SHOE - STAY BIG ON TIE FOR THIS HAND ; IF NO TIE REPEAT REDUCE BET

8 IN A ROW ON BANK - STAY WITH THE STREAK

Bet $ BANK: 450	Bet $ PLAYER:			Bet $ TIE: 200	
PLAYER Cards:	K	9	—	Total: 9	
BANK Cards:	4	A	—	Total: 5	
Result:	BANK:		PLAYER: ✓	TIE:	
Cumul. Score:	BANK: 13		PLAYER: 6	TIE: 8	
Cumulative Win / (Loss) $: +2885					

Hand Number: 28

Trend / Pattern: TIE PATTERNS ; POTENTIAL SWITCH-OVER TO PLAYER

Bet Selection Method: PATTERN TIE REPEATS ; SAME AS LAST DECISION

Bet Progression: MEDIUM PATTERN TIE REPEATS ; MEDIUM TRIPLE 2-3-2 AT $100/UNIT

Rationale / Comments: I WILL BET TIE FOR 4 MORE HANDS LOOKING FOR A REPEAT ON THE 4TH (THE 5TH DECISION AFTER TIE - 8)

WITH THE LAST LOSS I AM MORE CONSERVATIVE ; SOMETIMES THE STREAK CAN SWITCH

Bet $ BANK:	Bet $ PLAYER: 200			Bet $ TIE: 50	
PLAYER Cards:	3	3	—	Total: 6	
BANK Cards:	A	A	8	Total: 0	
Result:	BANK:		PLAYER: ✓	TIE:	
Cumul. Score:	BANK: 13		PLAYER: 7	TIE: 8	
Cumulative Win / (Loss) $: + 3035					

Hand Number: **29**

Trend / Pattern: *TIE PATTERNS, POSSIBLE PLAYER WIN STREAK*

Bet Selection Method: *PATTERN TIE REPEATS, SAME AS LAST DECISION*

Bet Progression: *SAME FOR TIE, SECOND BET OF MEDIUM TRIPLE 2-3-2*

Rationale / Comments: *3 MORE TIE BETS*

PLAYER HAS WON 2 STRAIGHT, THIS DECISION IF PLAYER WILL LIKELY INDICATE A WIN STREAK OPPORTUNITY

Bet $ BANK:	Bet $ PLAYER: 300			Bet $ TIE: 50	
PLAYER Cards:	8	10	—	Total:	8
BANK Cards:	K	4	—	Total:	4
Result:	BANK:		PLAYER: ✓	TIE:	
Cumul. Score:	BANK: 13		PLAYER: 8	TIE:	8
Cumulative Win / (Loss) $: +3285					

Hand Number: **30**

Trend / Pattern: *TIE PATTERNS, PLAYER WIN STREAK*

Bet Selection Method: *PATTERN TIE REPEATS, SAME AS LAST DECISION*

Bet Progression: *SAME FOR TIE, THIRD BET OF MEDIUM TRIPLE UPGRADED TO $150/UNIT*

Rationale / Comments: *2 MORE TIE BETS*

3 IN A ROW FOR PLAYER — STREAK LOOKS GOOD, COULD MATCH BANK SO I UPGRADE BET

Bet $ BANK:	Bet $ PLAYER: 300			Bet $ TIE: 50	
PLAYER Cards:	J	5	3	Total:	8
BANK Cards:	7	Q	—	Total:	7
Result:	BANK:		PLAYER: ✓	TIE:	
Cumul. Score:	BANK: 13		PLAYER: 9	TIE:	8
Cumulative Win / (Loss) $: + 3535					

Hand Number: 31

Trend / Pattern: TIE PATTERNS; PLAYER WIN STREAK

Bet Selection Method: PATTERN TIE REPEATS; SAME AS LAST DECISION

Bet Progression: SAME TIE BUT UPGRADED: AGGRESSIVE TRIPLE 3-6-5 AT $150/UNIT

Rationale / Comments: THERE WERE 4 DECISIONS SINCE TIE-8, A TIE HERE WILL BE THE THIRD REPEAT OF THE PATTERN OF TIES WITH 4 DECISIONS BETWEEN THEM - I TRIPLE THIS BET

4 IN A ROW FOR PLAYER - I LOOK FOR 4 MORE

Bet $ BANK:	Bet $ PLAYER: 450			Bet $ TIE: 150	
PLAYER Cards:	9	K	—	Total:	9
BANK Cards:	6	6	—	Total:	2
Result:	BANK:		PLAYER: ✓	TIE:	
Cumul. Score:	BANK: 13		PLAYER: 10	TIE: 8	
Cumulative Win / (Loss) $: +3835					

Hand Number: 32

Trend / Pattern: PLAYER WIN STREAK

Bet Selection Method: SAME AS LAST DECISION

Bet Progression: SECOND BET OF AGGRESSIVE TRIPLE

Rationale / Comments: I GET OFF TIE'S UNTIL ANOTHER TIE OUTCOME

5 STRAIGHT FOR PLAYER - I WILL BE VERY AGGRESSIVE FOR NEXT 3 DECISIONS

Bet $ BANK:	Bet $ PLAYER: 900			Bet $ TIE:	
PLAYER Cards:	7	2	—	Total:	9
BANK Cards:	2	5	—	Total:	7
Result:	BANK:		PLAYER: ✓	TIE:	
Cumul. Score:	BANK: 13		PLAYER: 11	TIE: 8	
Cumulative Win / (Loss) $: +4735					

Hand Number: 33

Trend / Pattern: *PLAYER WIN STREAK*

Bet Selection Method: *SAME AS LAST DECISION*

Bet Progression: *AGGRESSIVE TRIPLE 3-6-5, LAST BET*

Rationale / Comments:

6 IN A ROW FOR PLAYER — LOOKING FOR PLAYER TO WIN 8 AND MATCH THE BANK WIN STREAK.

Bet $ BANK:	Bet $ PLAYER: 750		Bet $ TIE:	
PLAYER Cards:	4	9	A	Total: 4
BANK Cards:	7	5	9	Total: 1
Result:	BANK:	PLAYER: ✓	TIE:	
Cumul. Score:	BANK: 13	PLAYER: 12	TIE: 8	
Cumulative Win / (Loss) $: + 5485				

Hand Number: 34

Trend / Pattern: *PLAYER WIN STREAK*

Bet Selection Method: *SAME AS LAST DECISION*

Bet Progression: *AGGRESSIVE DOUBLE 4-2 AT $250/UNIT*

Rationale / Comments:

7 STRAIGHT — A WIN MATCHES THE BANK STREAK OF 8

Bet $ BANK:	Bet $ PLAYER: 1000		Bet $ TIE:	
PLAYER Cards:	6	4	—	Total: 7
BANK Cards:	A	10	2	Total: 3
Result:	BANK:	PLAYER: ✓	TIE:	
Cumul. Score:	BANK: 13	PLAYER: 13	TIE: 8	
Cumulative Win / (Loss) $: + 6485				

Hand Number: 35

Trend / Pattern: PLAYER WIN STREAK

Bet Selection Method: OPPOSITE LAST DECISION

Bet Progression: AGGRESSIVE DOUBLE 4-2 SECOND BET

Rationale / Comments: DECISION: DO I BET THAT THE PLAYER STREAK WILL CONTINUE, OR JUST MATCH THE 8 STRAIGHT BY BANK?

I DECIDE TO SWITCH TO BANK — I ONLY DO THIS FOR MATCHES OTHERWISE I WOULD STAY PLAYER

Bet $ BANK: 500	Bet $ PLAYER:			Bet $ TIE:	
PLAYER Cards:	6	8	—	Total:	4
BANK Cards:	8	Q	—	Total:	8
Result:	BANK: ✓		PLAYER:	TIE:	
Cumul. Score:	BANK: 14		PLAYER: 13	TIE: 8	
Cumulative Win / (Loss) $: + 6985					

Hand Number: 36

Trend / Pattern: POSSIBLE SWITCH TO BANK

Bet Selection Method: SAME AS LAST DECISION

Bet Progression: MEDIUM DOUBLE 2-3 AT $300 PER UNIT

Rationale / Comments: I WAS RIGHT ON THE LAST HAND SWITCH, BUT NOW WHAT? I STAY WITH BANK

Bet $ BANK: 600	Bet $ PLAYER:			Bet $ TIE:	
PLAYER Cards:	J	5	J	Total:	5
BANK Cards:	3	9	8	Total:	0
Result:	BANK:		PLAYER: ✓	TIE:	
Cumul. Score:	BANK: 14		PLAYER: 14	TIE: 8	
Cumulative Win / (Loss) $: + 6385					

Hand Number: 37

Trend / Pattern: REPETITIVE PATTERN

Bet Selection Method: OPPOSITE LAST DECISION

Bet Progression: MEDIUM DOUBLE 2-3 AT $300 SAME FIRST BET

Rationale / Comments: AFTER MATCHING WIN STREAKS OF 8, THE TREND SEEMS TO BE BACK TO AN ALTERNATING PATTERN — HOPEFULLY IT WILL BE REPETITIVE. I SWITCH TO BANK — A SWITCH BASED ON LAST PLAYER WIN

Bet $ BANK: 600	Bet $ PLAYER:		Bet $ TIE:	
PLAYER Cards:	3	Q	Q	Total: 3
BANK Cards:	6	4	Q	Total: 0
Result:	BANK:	PLAYER: ✓	TIE:	
Cumul. Score:	BANK: 14	PLAYER: 15	TIE: 8	
Cumulative Win / (Loss) $: +5785				

Hand Number: 38

Trend / Pattern: POSSIBLE PLAYER WIN STREAK OR REPETITIVE PATTERN

Bet Selection Method: SAME AS LAST DECISION

Bet Progression: SAME MEDIUM DOUBLE 2-3 DOWNGRADED TO $200/UNIT

Rationale / Comments: DECISION! PLAYER STREAK OR ALTERNATING SHORT WINS. PLAYER HAS WON THE LAST 2 DECISIONS, I DECIDE TO BET PLAYER

Bet $ BANK:	Bet $ PLAYER: 200		Bet $ TIE:	
PLAYER Cards:	A	K	9	Total: 0
BANK Cards:	6	A	—	Total: 7
Result:	BANK: ✓	PLAYER:	TIE:	
Cumul. Score:	BANK: 15	PLAYER: 15	TIE: 8	
Cumulative Win / (Loss) $: + 5385				

Hand Number: 39

Trend / Pattern: REPETITIVE PATTERN

Bet Selection Method: NO BET

Bet Progression: NOT APPLICABLE

Rationale / Comments: AFTER 3 STRAIGHT LOSSES, I SIT-OUT A FEW HANDS TO SEE WHAT DEVELOPS.

THE PATTERN SEEMS TO BE B-P-P

Bet $ BANK: 0	Bet $ PLAYER: 0		Bet $ TIE: 0	
PLAYER Cards:	Q	J	6	Total: 6
BANK Cards:	A	K	10	Total: 1
Result:	BANK:	PLAYER: ✓	TIE:	
Cumul. Score:	BANK: 15	PLAYER: 16	TIE: 8	
Cumulative Win / (Loss) $: +5385				

Hand Number: 40

Trend / Pattern: REPETITIVE PATTERN

Bet Selection Method: NO BET

Bet Progression: NOT APPLICABLE

Rationale / Comments: SO FAR B-P-P PATTERN; IF SO THE NEXT DECISION SHOULD BE PLAYER

Bet $ BANK: 0	Bet $ PLAYER: 0		Bet $ TIE: 0	
PLAYER Cards:	A	K	2	Total: 3
BANK Cards:	A	A	2	Total: 4
Result:	BANK: ✓	PLAYER:	TIE:	
Cumul. Score:	BANK: 16	PLAYER: 16	TIE: 8	
Cumulative Win / (Loss) $: +5385				

Hand Number: 41

Trend / Pattern: REPETITIVE PATTERN

Bet Selection Method: NO BET

Bet Progression: NOT APPLICABLE

Rationale / Comments: SINCE HAND 35 THE PATTERN HAS BEEN B-P-P-B-P-B BANK WON HAND 40, SO IF THERE IS A REPETITIVE, PLAYER SHOULD WIN THIS AND THE NEXT DECISION.

Bet $ BANK: 0	Bet $ PLAYER: 0		Bet $ TIE: 0	
PLAYER Cards:	8	K	—	Total: 8
BANK Cards:	10	7	—	Total: 7
Result:	BANK:	PLAYER: ✓	TIE:	
Cumul. Score:	BANK: 16	PLAYER: 17	TIE: 8	
Cumulative Win / (Loss) $: + 5385				

Hand Number: 42

Trend / Pattern: REPETITIVE PATTERN

Bet Selection Method: SAME AS LAST DECISION

Bet Progression: MEDIUM TRIPLE 2-3-2 AT $200/UNIT

Rationale / Comments: SINCE PLAYER WON THE LAST DECISION, I AM LOOKING FOR THE PATTERN OF 5 DECISIONS, B-P-P-B-P, TO REPEAT. SO FAR IT HAS FOR THE FIRST 2 DECISIONS, I BET PLAYER

Bet $ BANK:	Bet $ PLAYER: 400		Bet $ TIE:	
PLAYER Cards:	K	8	—	Total: 8
BANK Cards:	J	7	—	Total: 7
Result:	BANK:	PLAYER: ✓	TIE:	
Cumul. Score:	BANK: 16	PLAYER: 18	TIE: 8	
Cumulative Win / (Loss) $: + 5785				

Hand Number: 43

Trend / Pattern: REPETITIVE PATTERN

Bet Selection Method: OPPOSITE LAST DECISION

Bet Progression: SECOND BET OF MEDIUM TRIPLE 2-3-2 AT $200/UNIT

Rationale / Comments: FOLLOWING THE PATTERN, THE LAST 3 DECISIONS WERE B-P-P; THE NEXT 2 SHOULD BE B-P FOR A REPEAT OF HANDS 35-39.

Bet $ BANK: 600	Bet $ PLAYER:			Bet $ TIE:	
PLAYER Cards:	4	7	J	Total:	1
BANK Cards:	10	3	10	Total:	3
Result:	BANK: ✓		PLAYER:	TIE:	
Cumul. Score:	BANK: 17		PLAYER: 18	TIE: 8	
Cumulative Win / (Loss) $: + 6385					

Hand Number: 44

Trend / Pattern: REPETITIVE PATTERN

Bet Selection Method: OPPOSITE LAST DECISION

Bet Progression: LAST BET OF THE MEDIUM TRIPLE

Rationale / Comments: A PLAYER WIN HERE WILL COMPLETE THE REPEAT

Bet $ BANK:	Bet $ PLAYER: 400			Bet $ TIE:	
PLAYER Cards:	8	Q	—	Total:	8
BANK Cards:	8	4	—	Total:	2
Result:	BANK:		PLAYER: ✓	TIE:	
Cumul. Score:	BANK: 17		PLAYER: 19	TIE: 8	
Cumulative Win / (Loss) $: + 6785					

Hand Number: 45

Trend / Pattern: REPETITIVE PATTERN

Bet Selection Method: OPPOSITE LAST DECISION

Bet Progression: AGGRESSIVE DOUBLE 3-5 AT $200/UNIT

Rationale / Comments: THE 5 DECISION PATTERN IN HANDS 35-39 REPEATED FOR 40-44 A SECOND REPEAT WOULD BE UNUSAL, BUT I MUST FOLLOW THE FLOW

Bet $ BANK: 600	Bet $ PLAYER:			Bet $ TIE:	
PLAYER Cards:	K	Q	3	Total: 3	
BANK Cards:	9	3	4	Total: 6	
Result:	BANK: ✓		PLAYER:	TIE:	
Cumul. Score:	BANK: 18		PLAYER: 19	TIE: 8	
Cumulative Win / (Loss) $: +7385					

Hand Number: 46

Trend / Pattern: REPETITIVE PATTERN

Bet Selection Method: OPPOSITE LAST DECISION

Bet Progression: SECOND BET OF THE AGGRESSIVE DOUBLE 3-5

Rationale / Comments: IF THE PATTERN REPEATS THIS AND THE NEXT DECISION SHOULD BE PLAYER

Bet $ BANK:	Bet $ PLAYER: 1000			Bet $ TIE:	
PLAYER Cards:	10	J	2	Total: 2	
BANK Cards:	10	Q	J	Total: 0	
Result:	BANK:		PLAYER: ✓	TIE:	
Cumul. Score:	BANK: 18		PLAYER: 20	TIE: 8	
Cumulative Win / (Loss) $: +8385					

Hand Number: 47

Trend / Pattern: REPETITIVE PATTERN

Bet Selection Method: SAME AS LAST DECISION

Bet Progression: AGGRESSIVE TRIPLE 3-6-5 AT $300/UNIT

Rationale / Comments: SO FAR SO GOOD FOR THE SECOND REPEAT, THE FIRST 2 DECISIONS HAVE BEEN RIGHT ON IT. I AM LOOKING TO COMPLETE THE REPEAT, SO THE NEXT 3 DECISIONS SHOULD BE P-B-P

Bet $ BANK:	Bet $ PLAYER: 900		Bet $ TIE:	
PLAYER Cards:	4	4	—	Total: 8
BANK Cards:	7	3	—	Total: 0
Result:	BANK:	PLAYER: ✓	TIE:	
Cumul. Score:	BANK: 18	PLAYER: 21	TIE: 8	
Cumulative Win / (Loss) $: + 9285				

Hand Number: 48

Trend / Pattern: REPETITIVE PATTERN

Bet Selection Method: OPPOSITE LAST DECISION

Bet Progression: SECOND BET OF THE TRIPLE 3-6-5

Rationale / Comments: 3 OF THE FIVE-DECISION PATTERN HAVE COME, LOOKING FOR THE NEXT 2 — B-P.

THIS IS A BIG BET — NORMALLY I WOULD NOT BE AS AGGRESSIVE

Bet $ BANK: 1800	Bet $ PLAYER:		Bet $ TIE:	
PLAYER Cards:	K	5	3	Total: 8
BANK Cards:	4	6	K	Total: 0
Result:	BANK:	PLAYER: ✓	TIE:	
Cumul. Score:	BANK: 18	PLAYER: 22	TIE: 8	
Cumulative Win / (Loss) $: + 7485				

Hand Number: 49

Trend / Pattern: POSSIBLE PLAYER WIN STREAK

Bet Selection Method: SAME AS LAST DECISION

Bet Progression: MEDIUM DOUBLE 1-3 AT $500/UNIT

Rationale / Comments: THE SECOND REPEAT OF THE 5-DECISION PATTERN DID NOT OCCUR — ONLY A PARTIAL REPEAT OF 3 OF THE 5 DECISIONS THE LAST LOSS WAS LARGE AND I SHOULD HAVE BEEN MORE CONSERVATIVE. 3 STRAIGHT FOR PLAYER

Bet $ BANK:	Bet $ PLAYER: 500			Bet $ TIE:	
PLAYER Cards:	K	Q	3	Total: 3	
BANK Cards:	5	10	—	Total: 5	
Result:	BANK: ✓		PLAYER:	TIE:	
Cumul. Score:	BANK: 19		PLAYER: 22	TIE: 8	
Cumulative Win / (Loss) $: +6985					

Hand Number: 50

Trend / Pattern: REPETITIVE PATTERN

Bet Selection Method: OPPOSITE LAST DECISION

Bet Progression: MEDIUM DOUBLE 1-3 DOWNLOADED TO $300/UNIT — FIRST BET

Rationale / Comments: THE LAST 2 LOSSES HURT SO I CUT BACK AND REMAIN MORE CONSERVATIVE. IF I FALL BACK BELOW +6000 I WILL QUIT. PLAYER WON 3 STRAIGHT FOLLOWED BY A BANK WIN — I GO WITH PLAYER

Bet $ BANK:	Bet $ PLAYER: 300			Bet $ TIE:	
PLAYER Cards:	9	7	—	Total: 6	
BANK Cards:	3	5	—	Total: 8	
Result:	BANK: ✓		PLAYER:	TIE:	
Cumul. Score:	BANK: 20		PLAYER: 22	TIE: 8	
Cumulative Win / (Loss) $: +6685					

Hand Number: 51

Trend / Pattern: REPETITIVE PATTERN

Bet Selection Method: SAME AS LAST DECISION

Bet Progression: MEDIUM DOUBLE 1-3 AT $300 PER UNIT

Rationale / Comments: THE SECOND WIN BY BANK INDICATES A MATCHING 3-WIN A SIDE PATTERN.

Bet $ BANK: 300	Bet $ PLAYER:			Bet $ TIE:	
PLAYER Cards:	A	5	–	Total:	6
BANK Cards:	K	8	–	Total:	8
Result:	BANK: ✓		PLAYER:	TIE:	
Cumul. Score:	BANK: 21		PLAYER: 22	TIE: 8	
Cumulative Win / (Loss) $: +6985					

Hand Number: 52

Trend / Pattern: REPETITIVE PATTERN

Bet Selection Method: OPPOSITE LAST DECISION

Bet Progression: SECOND BET OF MEDIUM DOUBLE 1-3

Rationale / Comments: SWITCH BACK TO PLAYER LOOKING FOR ANOTHER 3 WINS

Bet $ BANK:	Bet $ PLAYER: 900			Bet $ TIE:	
PLAYER Cards:	Q	Q	7	Total:	7
BANK Cards:	6	10	4	Total:	7
Result:	BANK:		PLAYER:	TIE: ✓	
Cumul. Score:	BANK: 21		PLAYER: 22	TIE: 9	
Cumulative Win / (Loss) $: +6985					

Hand Number: 53

Trend / Pattern: REPETITIVE PATTERN

Bet Selection Method: TIE AFTER TIE ; OPPOSITE THE DECISION BEFORE TIE

Bet Progression: TIE AFTER TIE DOUBLE UP ; AGGRESSIVE TRIPLE AT $300/UNIT — 3-6-5

Rationale / Comments: THE LAST TIE WIN WAS A $100 BET — I DOUBLE UP TO $200

NORMALLY I WOULD STAY WITH BANK AFTER 3 STRAIGHT WINS BEFORE A TIE, BUT I AM FOLLOWING A 3-WINS-A-SIDE PATTERN

Bet $ BANK:	Bet $ PLAYER: 900		Bet $ TIE: 200	
PLAYER Cards:	8	2	6	Total: 6
BANK Cards:	3	J	3	Total: 6
Result:	BANK:	PLAYER:	TIE: ✓	
Cumul. Score:	BANK: 21	PLAYER: 22	TIE: 10	
Cumulative Win / (Loss) $: + 8585				

Hand Number: 54

Trend / Pattern: REPETITIVE PATTERN

Bet Selection Method: TIE AFTER TIE ; OPPOSITE THE DECISION BEFORE TIE

Bet Progression: SAME TRIPLE FIRST BET ; TIE AFTER TIE 50% INCREASE

Rationale / Comments: LOOKING FOR A THIRD TIE

I STAY WITH THE 3-A SIDE PATTERN

Bet $ BANK:	Bet $ PLAYER: 900		Bet $ TIE: 300	
PLAYER Cards:	9	Q	—	Total: 9
BANK Cards:	2	K	—	Total: 2
Result:	BANK:	PLAYER: ✓	TIE:	
Cumul. Score:	BANK: 21	PLAYER: 23	TIE: 10	
Cumulative Win / (Loss) $: + 9185				

Hand Number: 55

Trend / Pattern: REPETITIVE PATTERN

Bet Selection Method: SAME AS LAST DECISION; BUNCHED TIE REPEATS

Bet Progression: AGGRESSIVE BUNCHED TIES, 4 UNITS AT $25 PER; SECOND BET OF TRIPLE 3-6-5 AT $300/PER

Rationale / Comments: I WILL BET TIE FOR 4 DECISIONS LOOKING FOR A REPEAT

LOOKING FOR 2 MORE PLAYER WINS TO REPEAT THE 3-A SIDE PATTERN

Bet $ BANK:	Bet $ PLAYER: 1800		Bet $ TIE: 100	
PLAYER Cards:	7	10	—	Total: 7
BANK Cards:	A	7	—	Total: 8
Result:	BANK: ✓	PLAYER:	TIE:	
Cumul. Score:	BANK: 22	PLAYER: 23	TIE: 10	
Cumulative Win / (Loss) $: + 7285				

Hand Number: 56

Trend / Pattern: REPETITIVE PATTERN

Bet Selection Method: OPPOSITE LAST DECISION; BUNCHED TIE REPEATS

Bet Progression: SAME ON TIE; MEDIUM DOUBLE 1-3 AT $500/UNIT

Rationale / Comments: 3 MORE TIE BETS

AFTER ANOTHER LARGE-BET LOSS I ALWAYS CUT BACK AGGRESSIVELY. I CAN ALWAYS RELOAD LATER. LOOKING FOR AN ALTERNATING SINGLE WIN PATTERN — BACK ON PLAYER

Bet $ BANK:	Bet $ PLAYER: 500		Bet $ TIE: 100	
PLAYER Cards:	10	J	J	Total: 0
BANK Cards:	J	7	—	Total: 7
Result:	BANK: ✓	PLAYER:	TIE:	
Cumul. Score:	BANK: 23	PLAYER: 23	TIE: 10	
Cumulative Win / (Loss) $: + 6685				

Hand Number: 57

Trend / Pattern: REPETITIVE PATTERN

Bet Selection Method: SAME AS LAST DECISION! BUNCHED TIE REPEATS

Bet Progression: SAME TIE BET! SAME MEDIUM DOUBLE 1-3 AT $500/UNIT — FIRST BET

Rationale / Comments: 2 MORE TIE BETS

2 IN A ROW FOR BANK — LOOKING FOR A THIRD ON BANK

Bet $ BANK: 500	Bet $ PLAYER:			Bet $ TIE: 100	
PLAYER Cards:	8	5	4	Total: 7	
BANK Cards:	5	K	10	Total: 5	
Result:	BANK:		PLAYER: ✓	TIE:	
Cumul. Score:	BANK: 23		PLAYER: 24	TIE: 10	
Cumulative Win / (Loss) $: +6085					

Hand Number: 58

Trend / Pattern: REPETITIVE PATTERN

Bet Selection Method: OPPOSITE LAST DECISION! BUNCHED TIE REPEATS

Bet Progression: SAME TIE BET! SAME MEDIUM DOUBLE FIRST BET

Rationale / Comments: LAST TIE BET

BASED ON THE PATTERN P-B-B, I AM LOOKING FOR 2 BANK WINS TO REPEAT THE PATTERN. IF I LOSE THIS BET, I WILL CONSIDER SITTING OUT A FEW HANDS OR QUITING.

Bet $ BANK: 500	Bet $ PLAYER:			Bet $ TIE: 100	
PLAYER Cards:	9	8	—	Total: 7	
BANK Cards:	9	J	—	Total: 9	
Result:	BANK: ✓		PLAYER:	TIE:	
Cumul. Score:	BANK: 24		PLAYER: 24	TIE: 10	
Cumulative Win / (Loss) $: +6485					

Hand Number: 59

Trend / Pattern: REPETITIVE PATTERN

Bet Selection Method: SAME AS LAST DECISION

Bet Progression: SECOND BET OF MEDIUM DOUBLE 1-3 AT $500/UNIT

Rationale / Comments: OFF TIE'S UNTIL ANOTHER TIE A WIN HERE WILL COMPLETE THE REPEAT OF THE P-B-B PATTERN

Bet $ BANK: 1500	Bet $ PLAYER:			Bet $ TIE:	
PLAYER Cards:	10	A	Q	Total:	1
BANK Cards:	J	2	Q	Total:	2
Result:	BANK: ✓		PLAYER:	TIE:	
Cumul. Score:	BANK: 25		PLAYER: 24	TIE: 10	
Cumulative Win / (Loss) $: +7985					

Hand Number: 60

Trend / Pattern: REPETITIVE PATTERN

Bet Selection Method: OPPOSITE LAST DECISION

Bet Progression: AGGRESSIVE TRIPLE 4-2-3 AT $400 /UNIT

Rationale / Comments: THE LAST WIN COMPLETED THE REPEAT. LOOKING FOR A SECOND REPEAT SO I BET PLAYER

Bet $ BANK:	Bet $ PLAYER: 1600			Bet $ TIE:	
PLAYER Cards:	2	K	K	Total:	2
BANK Cards:	5	A	—	Total:	6
Result:	BANK: ✓		PLAYER:	TIE:	
Cumul. Score:	BANK: 26		PLAYER: 24	TIE: 10	
Cumulative Win / (Loss) $: + 6385					

Hand Number: 61

Trend / Pattern: REPETITIVE PATTERN OR POSSIBLE BANK WIN STREAK

Bet Selection Method: SAME AS LAST DECISION

Bet Progression: CONSERVATIVE TRIPLE 2-1-2 AT $250/UNIT

Rationale / Comments: THE LAST WIN MADE IT 3 FOR BANK - WILL THE PATTERN BE 3 A SIDE, A SINGLE PLAYER THEN BACK TO BANK, OR SS JT A BANK STREAK? I DECIDE TO GO WITH THE STREAK BUT STAY LOWER ON BET - THIS DECISION WILL DECIDE FUTURE BETS

Bet $ BANK: 500	Bet $ PLAYER:			Bet $ TIE:	
PLAYER Cards:	4	A	8	Total: 3	
BANK Cards:	K	2	5	Total: 7	
Result:	BANK: ✓		PLAYER:	TIE:	
Cumul. Score:	BANK: 27		PLAYER: 24	TIE: 10	
Cumulative Win / (Loss) $: +6885					

Hand Number: 62

Trend / Pattern: BANK WIN STREAK

Bet Selection Method: SAME AS LAST DECISION

Bet Progression: INTERCHANGE TO AGGRESSIVE TRIPLE 4-2-3 AT $250/UNIT

Rationale / Comments:

4 STRAIGHT FOR BANK - I HAVE TO STAY WITH BANK. THE 4TH WIN CONVINCED ME OF THE STREAK.

Bet $ BANK: 1000	Bet $ PLAYER:			Bet $ TIE:	
PLAYER Cards:	J	10	3	Total: 3	
BANK Cards:	A	3	10	Total: 4	
Result:	BANK: ✓		PLAYER:	TIE:	
Cumul. Score:	BANK: 28		PLAYER: 24	TIE: 10	
Cumulative Win / (Loss) $: +7885					

Hand Number: 63

Trend / Pattern: BANK WIN STREAK

Bet Selection Method: SAME AS LAST DECISION

Bet Progression: SECOND BET OF TRIPLE 4-2-3 UPGRADED TO $ 400/UNIT

Rationale / Comments:

5 IN A ROW MEANS I HAVE TO BE MORE AGGRESSIVE SO I INCREASE MY BET AMOUNT / UNIT

Bet $ BANK: 800	Bet $ PLAYER:			Bet $ TIE:	
PLAYER Cards:	J	4	—	Total:	4
BANK Cards:	8	10	—	Total:	8
Result:	BANK: ✓		PLAYER:	TIE:	
Cumul. Score:	BANK: 29		PLAYER: 24	TIE: 10	
Cumulative Win / (Loss) $: + 8685					

Hand Number: 64

Trend / Pattern: BANK WIN STREAK

Bet Selection Method: SAME AS LAST DECISION

Bet Progression: LAST BET OF UPGRADED TRIPLE

Rationale / Comments:

6 STRAIGHT FOR BANK

Bet $ BANK: 1200	Bet $ PLAYER:			Bet $ TIE:	
PLAYER Cards:	2	J	3	Total:	5
BANK Cards:	7	Q	—	Total:	7
Result:	BANK: ✓		PLAYER:	TIE:	
Cumul. Score:	BANK: 30		PLAYER: 24	TIE: 10	
Cumulative Win / (Loss) $: + 9885					

Hand Number: 65

Trend / Pattern: BANK WIN STREAK

Bet Selection Method: SAME AS LAST DECISION

Bet Progression: AGGRESSIVE DOUBLE 3-5 AT
$300 / UNIT

Rationale / Comments:

7 IN A ROW FOR BANK — STAY AGGRESSIVE
BUT STILL CONSERVE SOME PROFIT

Bet $ BANK: 900	Bet $ PLAYER:			Bet $ TIE:	
PLAYER Cards:	8	8	—	Total:	6
BANK Cards:	K	4	A	Total:	5
Result:	BANK:		PLAYER: ✓	TIE:	
Cumul. Score:	BANK: 30		PLAYER: 25	TIE: 10	
Cumulative Win / (Loss) $: +8985					

Hand Number: 66

Trend / Pattern: REPETITIVE PATTERN

Bet Selection Method: SAME AS LAST DECISION

Bet Progression: AGGRESSIVE DOUBLE 3-5 DOWN
TO $200/UNIT

Rationale / Comments: DOWNGRADE BET AFTER
LARGE BET LOSS. IF PLAYER WIN STREAK
OCCURS I CAN ALSO UPGRADE AGAIN.

POSSIBLE PLAYER MATCHING STREAK
AS BEFORE — BUT BE CONSERVATIVE

Bet $ BANK:	Bet $ PLAYER: 600			Bet $ TIE:	
PLAYER Cards:	4	7	4	Total:	5
BANK Cards:	10	5	10	Total:	0
Result:	BANK:		PLAYER: ✓	TIE:	
Cumul. Score:	BANK: 30		PLAYER: 26	TIE: 10	
Cumulative Win / (Loss) $: +9585					

Hand Number: 67

Trend / Pattern: POTENTIAL PLAYER WIN STREAK

Bet Selection Method: SAME AS LAST DECISION

Bet Progression: SECOND BET OF DOUBLE BUT DOWN TO $150/UNIT

Rationale / Comments: NORMALLY I WAIT FOR 3 IN A ROW BEFORE GETTING TO ABANGESSIVE. I DOWN GRADE BUT STAY ON PLAYER

Bet $ BANK:	Bet $ PLAYER: 750			Bet $ TIE:	
PLAYER Cards:	8	8	-	Total: 6	
BANK Cards:	5	9	3	Total: 7	
Result:	BANK: ✓		PLAYER:	TIE:	
Cumul. Score:	BANK: 31		PLAYER: 26	TIE: 10	
Cumulative Win / (Loss) $: + 8835					

Hand Number: 68

Trend / Pattern: REPETITIVE PATTERN

Bet Selection Method: SAME AS LAST DECISION

Bet Progression: MEDIUM DOUBLE 1-3 AT $500/UNIT

Rationale / Comments: BACK TO ALTERNATING SHORT WIN REPEATS — THE PLAYER WIN STREAK DID NOT OCCUR. LOOKING FOR ANOTHER BANK WIN TO MATCH THE 2 PLAYER WINS

Bet $ BANK: 500	Bet $ PLAYER:			Bet $ TIE:	
PLAYER Cards:	9	2	4	Total: 5	
BANK Cards:	7	5	3	Total: 5	
Result:	BANK:		PLAYER:	TIE: ✓	
Cumul. Score:	BANK: 31		PLAYER: 26	TIE: 11	
Cumulative Win / (Loss) $: + 8835					

Hand Number: 69

Trend / Pattern: REPETITIVE PATTERN

Bet Selection Method: TIE AFTER TIE ; FOLLOW BANK

Bet Progression: SAME MEDIUM DOUBLE 1-3 AT $500/UNIT ; TIE AFTER TIE

Rationale / Comments: BET TIE SAME AS LAST TIE WIN FOR $200

INSTEAD OF OPPOSITE THE DECISION BEFORE TIE, I USE FOLLOW BANK SINCE I AM LOOKING FOR A SECOND BANK WIN TO MATCH 2 PLAYER WINS

	BANK	PLAYER			TIE
Bet $ BANK: 500	Bet $ PLAYER:				Bet $ TIE: 200
PLAYER Cards:	8	2	Q	Total:	0
BANK Cards:	Q	J	9	Total:	9
Result:	BANK: ✓	PLAYER:		TIE:	
Cumul. Score:	BANK: 32	PLAYER: 26		TIE: 11	
Cumulative Win / (Loss) $: +9135					

Hand Number: 70

Trend / Pattern: REPETITIVE PATTERN ; TIE PATTERNS

Bet Selection Method: OPPOSITE LAST DECISION ; BUNCHED TIE REPEATS

Bet Progression: SECOND BET OF 1-3 DOUBLE ; AGGRESSIVE BUNCHED TIES - 4 UNITS $50/UNIT

Rationale / Comments: AGAIN I WILL MAKE 4 MORE TIE BETS LOOKING FOR A REPEAT WITHIN NEXT 4 DECISIONS

ALTERNATING DOUBLE WIN PATTERN - LOOKING FOR 2 PLAYER WINS

	BANK	PLAYER			TIE
Bet $ BANK:	Bet $ PLAYER: 1500				Bet $ TIE: 200
PLAYER Cards:	J	3	2	Total:	5
BANK Cards:	3	2	—	Total:	5
Result:	BANK:	PLAYER:		TIE: ✓	
Cumul. Score:	BANK: 32	PLAYER: 26		TIE: 12	
Cumulative Win / (Loss) $: +10735					

Hand Number: 71

Trend / Pattern: REPETITIVE PATTERN ; TIE PATTERNS

Bet Selection Method: OPPOSITE THE DECISION BEFORE TIE ; TIE AFTER TIE

Bet Progression: SECOND BET OF SAME DOUBLE ; TIE AFTER TIE - 50% INCREASE

Rationale / Comments: I ADD $100 TO THE TIE AND LOOK FOR 2 PLAYER WINS

Bet $ BANK:	Bet $ PLAYER: 1500			Bet $ TIE: 300	
PLAYER Cards:	4	5	—	Total:	9
BANK Cards:	10	3	—	Total:	3
Result:	BANK:		PLAYER: ✓	TIE:	
Cumul. Score:	BANK: 32		PLAYER: 27	TIE: 12	
Cumulative Win / (Loss) $: +11935					

Hand Number: 72

Trend / Pattern: REPETITIVE PATTERN ; TIE PATTERNS

Bet Selection Method: SAME AS LAST DECISION ; BUNCHED TIE REPEATS

Bet Progression: AGGRESSIVE DOUBLE 3-5 AT $500 PER UNIT ; AGGRESSIVE BUNCHED TIES $75/UNIT

Rationale / Comments: THERE WAS ONLY 1 DECISION BETWEEN TIE-11 AND 12 ; I AM LOOKING FOR ANOTHER TIE WITHIN THE NEXT 3 DECISIONS

BETTING ON A SECOND PLAYER WIN TO FOLLOW THE ALTERNATING DOUBLE WIN PATTERN

Bet $ BANK:	Bet $ PLAYER: 1500			Bet $ TIE: 300	
PLAYER Cards:	9	Q	—	Total:	9
BANK Cards:	A	8	—	Total:	9
Result:	BANK:		PLAYER:	TIE: ✓	
Cumul. Score:	BANK: 32		PLAYER: 27	TIE: 13	
Cumulative Win / (Loss) $: + 14335					

Hand Number: 73

Trend / Pattern: REPETITIVE PATTERN ; TIE PATTERNS

Bet Selection Method: TIE AFTER TIE ; FOLLOW PLAYER

Bet Progression: TIE AFTER TIE 50% INCREASE ; FIRST BET OF THE SAME DOUBLE 3-5 AT $500/UNIT

Rationale / Comments: ADD $150 TO LAST TIE BET - I SOME CASINO'S THE MAX ON TIE'S IS $400

LOOKING FOR A SECOND PLAYER WIN TO CONTINUE THE PATTERN - THUS I DID NOT USE OPPOSITE THE DECISION BEFORE TIE

Bet $ BANK:	Bet $ PLAYER: 1500		Bet $ TIE: 450	
PLAYER Cards:	5	6	—	Total: 1
BANK Cards:	7	A	—	Total: 8
Result:	BANK: ✓	PLAYER:	TIE:	
Cumul. Score:	BANK: 33	PLAYER: 27	TIE: 13	
Cumulative Win / (Loss) $: + 12,385				

Hand Number: 74

Trend / Pattern: REPETITIVE PATTERN ; TIE PATTERNS

Bet Selection Method: OPPOSITE LAST DECISION ; BUNCHED TIE REPEATS

Bet Progression: AGGRESSIVE BUNCHED TIES $50/UNIT ; CONSERVATIVE DOUBLE 2-1 AT $500/UNIT

Rationale / Comments: WITH THE LARGE LOSS ON THE LAST HAND I CUT BACK EVEN THOUGH A TIE REPEAT IS POSSIBLE - WITH 13 TIE'S I DECIDE TO BET TIE FOR NEXT 4 DECISIONS AT SAME $

I LOOK FOR A SINGLE WIN ON PLAYER

Bet $ BANK:	Bet $ PLAYER: 1000		Bet $ TIE: 200	
PLAYER Cards:	4	7	7	Total: 8
BANK Cards:	10	5	10	Total: 5
Result:	BANK:	PLAYER: ✓	TIE:	
Cumul. Score:	BANK: 33	PLAYER: 28	TIE: 13	
Cumulative Win / (Loss) $: + 13,185				

Hand Number: 75

Trend / Pattern: REPETITIVE PATTERN ; TIE PATTERNS

Bet Selection Method: OPPOSITE LAST DECISION; BUNCHED TIE REPEATS

Bet Progression: SAME TIE BET ; SECOND BET ON 2-1 DOUBLE

Rationale / Comments: SECOND TIE BET OF 4

LOOKING FOR A SINGLE WIN ON BANK TO FOLLOW THE ALTERNATING AND MATCHING WIN PATTERN

Bet $ BANK: 500	Bet $ PLAYER:			Bet $ TIE: 200	
PLAYER Cards:	Q	9	—	Total:	9
BANK Cards:	9	3	—	Total:	2
Result:	BANK:		PLAYER: ✓	TIE:	
Cumul. Score:	BANK: 33		PLAYER: 29	TIE: 13	
Cumulative Win / (Loss) $: +12,485					

Hand Number: 76

Trend / Pattern: REPETITIVE PATTERN ; TIE PATTERNS

Bet Selection Method: OPPOSITE LAST DECISION; BUNCHED TIE REPEATS

Bet Progression: SAME TIE BET ; MEDIUM DOUBLE 1-3 AT $500/UNIT

Rationale / Comments: THIRD TIE BET OF 4

2 WINS BY PLAYER — I LOOK FOR 2 WINS ON BANK TO FOLLOW THE PATTERN

Bet $ BANK: 500	Bet $ PLAYER:			Bet $ TIE: 200	
PLAYER Cards:	4	K	5	Total:	9
BANK Cards:	5	2	—	Total:	7
Result:	BANK:		PLAYER: ✓	TIE:	
Cumul. Score:	BANK: 33		PLAYER: 30	TIE: 13	
Cumulative Win / (Loss) $: +11,785					

Hand Number: 77

Trend / Pattern: POSSIBLE PLAYER WIN STREAK ; TIE PATTERNS

Bet Selection Method: SAME AS LAST DECISION ; BUNCHED TIE REPEATS

Bet Progression: SAME TIE BET ; AGGRESSIVE TRIPLE 3-6-5 AT $500/UNIT

Rationale / Comments: LAST TIE BET OF 4 3 IN A ROW FOR PLAYER — POSSIBLE WIN STREAK

ONLY A FEW HANDS LEFT IN THE SHOE

Bet $ BANK:	Bet $ PLAYER: 1500			Bet $ TIE: 200	
PLAYER Cards:	7	5	7	Total:	9
BANK Cards:	9	7	6	Total:	2
Result:	BANK:		PLAYER: ✔	TIE:	
Cumul. Score:	BANK: 33		PLAYER: 31	TIE: 13	
Cumulative Win / (Loss) $:	+ 13,085				

Hand Number: 78

Trend / Pattern: PLAYER WIN STREAK

Bet Selection Method: SAME AS LAST DECISION ; LATE TIES

Bet Progression: SECOND BET OF TRIPLE 3-6-5 ; AGGRESSIVE BUNCHED TIES $50/UNIT

Rationale / Comments: WITH A TIE-RICH SHOE AND ONLY A FEW HANDS LEFT I DECIDE TO BET TIE UNTIL THE END OF THE SHOE WITH A LARGE BET ON TIE ON THE LAST HAND.

4 IN A ROW FOR PLAYER — STAY LARGE ON FLOW

Bet $ BANK:	Bet $ PLAYER: 3000			Bet $ TIE: 200	
PLAYER Cards:	10	8	—	Total:	8
BANK Cards:	K	6	—	Total:	6
Result:	BANK:		PLAYER: ✔	TIE:	
Cumul. Score:	BANK: 33		PLAYER: 32	TIE: 13	
Cumulative Win / (Loss) $:	+ 15,885				

Hand Number: 79

Trend / Pattern: PLAYER WIN STREAK

Bet Selection Method: SAME AS LAST DECISION; LATE TIES

Bet Progression: LAST BET OF TRIPLE; SAME TIE BET

Rationale / Comments: CONTINUE TIE BETS

5 STRAIGHT FOR PLAYER — STAY ON TT

Bet $ BANK:	Bet $ PLAYER: 2500			Bet $ TIE: 200	
PLAYER Cards:	Q	2	7	Total:	9
BANK Cards:	J	6	9	Total:	5
Result:	BANK:		PLAYER: ✓	TIE:	
Cumul. Score:	BANK: 33		PLAYER: 33	TIE: 13	
Cumulative Win / (Loss) $:	+18,185				

Hand Number: 80

Trend / Pattern: PLAYER WIN STREAK

Bet Selection Method: SAME AS LAST DECISION; LAST HAND TIE

Bet Progression: AGGRESSIVE DOUBLE 3-5 AT $700 PER; AGGRESSIVE BUNCHED TIE $100/UNIT

Rationale / Comments: THE YELLOW MARKER SHOWED ON LAST HAND MEANING THIS IS THE LAST HAND OF THE SHOE. I DOUBLE UP ON THE TIE $200 TO $400.
USE THE LAST BET OF THE DOUBLE — 5 UNITS OR $3500

Bet $ BANK:	Bet $ PLAYER: 3500			Bet $ TIE: 400	
PLAYER Cards:	8	9	—	Total:	7
BANK Cards:	2	9	6	Total:	7
Result:	BANK:		PLAYER:	TIE: ✓	
Cumul. Score:	BANK: 33		PLAYER: 33	TIE: 14	
Cumulative Win / (Loss) $:	+21,385				

Summary and Analysis

The completed scorecards and following tables provide statistical summaries of the results of this Shoe.

The first table below is a scoring summary. Both BANK and PLAYER won 33 decisions. There were 80 total decisions and 14 TIE's.

Scoring Summary

BANK Wins: 33	PLAYER Wins: 33	TIE's: 14

Total Non-TIE Decisions	66
Total Decisions	80

The next table is a Won/Loss Bet Summary. I won fifty-five out of the total of 126 bets, for an overall winning bet percentage of 43.7%. The average winning bet was $712, but the average losing bet was only $311.

BANK/PLAYER Bets No Decision are bets made on BANK and PLAYER when the actual decision was a TIE. These fourteen bets on the BANK and PLAYER did not win or lose.

Won / Loss Bet Summary

Item	Number	$ Value
Winning Bets	55	39,135
BANK/PLAYER Winning Bets	43	28,215
Winning TIE Bets	12	10,920
$ Bet on Winning TIE's		1,365
BANK/PLAYER Bets No Decision	14	9,645
Losing Bets	57	17,750
Losing BANK/PLAYER Bets	20	13,800
Losing TIE Bets	37	3,950

HD #	Bet $	Circle Bets For	Cumul. $ Win/Loss	Score BK	Score PL
1	40/5	B/P/T	+35	①	
2	20/5	B/P/T	+75		TIE-1
3	50/10	B/P/T	+155		TIE-2
4	75/20	B/P/T	+210		①
5	50/10	B/P/T	+250	②	
6	75/10	B/P/T	+330		TIE-3
7	125/20	B/P/T	+435		②
8	100/20	B/P/T	+515	③	
9	100/40	B/P/T	+835		TIE-4
10	150/50	B/P/T	+635	4	
11	100/25	B/P/T	+835		TIE-5
12	150/50	B/P/T	+935		③
13	200/50	B/P/T	+685	5	
14	100/25	B/P/T	+560		4
15	100/25	B/P/T	+635		⑤
16	50/25	B/P/T	+835		TIE-6
17	150/50	B/P/T	+935	⑥	
18	225/25	B/P/T	+1135	⑦	
19	150/25	B/P/T	+960	8	
20	150/25	B/P/T	+1085	⑨	
21	250/50	B/P/T	+1485		TIE-7
22	225/50	B/P/T	+1660	⑩	
23	450/50	B/P/T	+2060	⑪	
24	375/50	B/P/T	+2385	⑫	
25	400/50	B/P/T	+2735	⑬	
26	200/100	B/P/T	+3535		TIE-8
27	450/200	B/P/T	+2885		6
28	200/50	B/P/T	+3035		⑦
29	300/50	B/P/T	+3285		⑧
30	300/50	B/P/T	+3535		⑨
31	450/150	B/P/T	+3835		⑩
32	900	B/P/T	+4735		⑪
33	750	B/P/T	+5485		⑫
34	1000	B/P/T	+6485		13
35	500	B/P/T	+6985	⑭	
36	600	B/P/T	+6385		14
37	600	B/P/T	+5785		15
38	400	B/P/T	+5385	15	
39	NO BET	B/P/T	+5385		16
40	NO BET	B/P/T	+5385	16	

HD #	Bet $	Circle Bets For	Cumul. $ Win/Loss	Score BK	PL
41	NO BET	B/P/T	+5385		17
42	400	B/P/T	+5785		18
43	600	B/P/T	+6385	17	
44	400	B/P/T	+6785		19
45	600	B/P/T	+7385	18	
46	1000	B/P/T	+8385		20
47	900	B/P/T	+9285		21
48	1800	B/P/T	+7485		22
49	500	B/P/T	+6985	19	
50	300	B/P/T	+6685	20	
51	300	B/P/T	+6985	21	
52	900	B/P/T	+6985		TIE-9
53	900/200	B/P/T	+8585	TIE-10	
54	900/300	B/P/T	+9185		23
55	1800/100	B/P/T	+7285	22	
56	500/100	B/P/T	+6685	23	
57	500/100	B/P/T	+6085		24
58	500/100	B/P/T	+6485	24	
59	1500	B/P/T	+7985	25	
60	1600	B/P/T	+6385	26	
61	500	B/P/T	+6885	27	
62	1000	B/P/T	+7885	28	
63	800	B/P/T	+8685	29	
64	1200	B/P/T	+9885	30	
65	900	B/P/T	+8985		25
66	600	B/P/T	+9585		26
67	750	B/P/T	+8835	31	
68	500	B/P/T	+8835		TIE-11
69	500/200	B/P/T	+9135	32	
70	1500/200	B/P/T	+10735	TIE-12	
71	1500/300	B/P/T	+11935		27
72	1500/300	B/P/T	+14335	TIE-13	
73	1500/450	B/P/T	+12385	33	
74	1000/200	B/P/T	+13185		28
75	500/200	B/P/T	+12485		29
76	500/200	B/P/T	+11785		30
77	1500/200	B/P/T	+13085		31
78	3000/200	B/P/T	+15885		32
79	2500/200	B/P/T	+18185		33
80	3500/400	B/P/T	+21385	TIE-14	

The table below highlights what a really great Shoe this turned out to be. Not accounting for the commissions on winning BANK bets, you would walk away from the table with over $22,000.

Starting Session Stake	$1,000
Total Dollars Won	$21,385
Percent Increase	2,138.5%

The Bet Summary table below is also very interesting. Notice that a total of 126 bets were made for nearly $57,000! The average size of each of these bets was over $450, an average of $671 for BANK and PLAYER bets combined, and an average $108 for TIE bets. The amount of money wagered on TIE's will always be considerably smaller.

Bet Summary

Bets Made	Number	$ Value
Total Action	126	56,975
On BANK	35	17,135
On PLAYER	42	34,525
Non-TIE Bet Total	77	51,660
Average Non-TIE Bet		671
On TIE's	49	5,315
Average TIE Bet		108
No Bet	3	0

Risk / Return Summary

Total Dollars Put at Risk	56,975
Total Dollars Won	39,135
Total Dollars Lost	17,750
Net Dollars Won	21,385
Total Return Percentage	37.5%

The Risk/Return Summary table shows a great return of 37.5%.

BANK, PLAYER and TIE Bet Summaries

The tables below provide separate wagering statistics for BANK, PLAYER and TIE.

BANK Bet Summary

BANK Bet Item	Number	$ Value
Total Bets	35	17,135
Average Bet $		490
Winning Bets	21	10,165
Average Winning Bet $		484
Losing Bets	9	5,950
Average Losing Bet $		661
Bets With TIE Result	5	1,020

BANK Bet Winning Percentage	70%

PLAYER Bet Summary

PLAYER Bet Item	Number	$ Value
Total Bets	42	34,525
Average Bet $		822
Winning Bets	22	18,050
Average Win Bet $		820
Losing Bets	11	7,850
Average Losing Bet $		714
Bets With TIE Result	9	8,625

PLAYER Bet Winning Percentage	67%

Notice some of the differences between the BANK and PLAYER Bet Summaries. More bets were made on PLAYER, but I won nearly the same number of bets on both. However, the bets on PLAYER were larger; on average 68% larger.

Winning bet percentages were similar for both. Note that the winning percentages were calculated based on the elimination of those bets made when the outcome was a TIE (5 bets for BANK and 9 bets for PLAYER). Therefore, I won 21 bets out of 30 on BANK, and 22 out of 33 on PLAYER. Overall, I won 43 bets out of the total of 63 (again eliminating the 14 bets made when a TIE decision occurred), for a winning percentage of 68.3%.

Referring to the TIE Bet Summary table, note that I made 49 TIE bets, quite a large number. This is not unusual for TIE-RICH Shoes such as this one. There were 14 TIE's, twice the typical number of seven, and I won 12.

TIE Bet Summary

TIE Bet Item	Number	$ Value
Total Bets	49	5,315
Average Bet $		108
Winning Bets	12	10,920
Average Win $ Per Bet		910
$ Bet on Winning TIE's		1,365
Losing Bets	37	3,950
Average Loss $ Per Bet		107

TIE Bet Winning Percentage	24.5%
TIE Bet Return Percentage	205.5%

Table 8 contains a summary of the kinds and numbers of opportunities provided in this Shoe. I had the advantage over the Casino in 60 out of the 80 total decisions. The six consecutive winning streak opportunities and the 24 TIE pattern advantages were the biggest moneymakers, accounting for nearly 80% of the total win.

Opportunity Summary

	Opportunity Classification	#	Total
1	Consecutive Winning Streaks of Three or More Decisions	6	35
2	Repetitive Patterns, One or More Repeats	3	12
3	Repeating TIE Patterns, Bunched TIE's	10	10
4	Repeating TIE Patterns, Pattern TIE's	7	7
5	Consecutive TIE's	2	2
6	First and Last TIE's	1	1
7	Early and Late TIE's	4	4
	Total Opportunities		71
	Adjusted Total Opportunities		60

Table 8

Lets review each of the seven opportunity classifications listed in table 8. Refer to the completed scorecards on pages 228 and 229.

1. Consecutive Winning Streaks of Three or more Decisions. There were 6 occurrences for a total of 35 decisions: BANK wins 6 to 13, PLAYER wins 6 to 13, PLAYER wins 20 to 22, BANK wins 19 to 21, BANK wins 24 to 30 and PLAYER wins 28 to 33. Notice that four of the six occurrences were matching consecutive win streaks. That is, the same number of wins on one side was immediately repeated on the other.

2. Repetitive Patterns of One or more Repeats. There were 3 occurrences for a total of 12 decisions:
   - One pair of alternating singles, BANK win number 2 and PLAYER win number 2, a repeat of the first wins for both.

- The outcome pattern of Hands 40 to 44 is a repeat of the pattern of Hands 35 to 39. The pattern of wins in this case is BANK, PLAYER, PLAYER, BANK and PLAYER. Unfortunately I missed some of it because I had stopped betting for three decisions. When I did recognize the opportunity I won six straight decisions. Notice I followed the same pattern again on Hands 45, 46, 47 and 48, but lost Hand 48 when a repeat of the full pattern did not materialize. The total number of opportunities from the pattern was 8, one full repeat of the pattern, plus a partial repeat.
- The final two opportunities was a repeat double; PLAYER wins 25 and 26, followed by BANK wins 31 and 32.

3. Repeating TIE Patterns, Bunched TIE's; 10 occurrences for a total of 10 decisions. These opportunities are TIE's that repeat within six decisions or less: TIE decisions 2, 3, 4, 5, 6, 7, 8, 10, 12 and 13.

4. Repeating TIE Patterns, TIE's that repeat with the same (or very nearly the same) number of decisions between them. There were 7 occurrences for 7 decisions. TIE decisions 2 and 3, and 3 and 4 occurred with two decisions each between them for two occurrences. Additionally, TIE decisions 5 and 6, and 7 and 8 had four decisions between them; there were three occurrences. And finally, TIE 11 and 12, and 12 and 13 had one decision between them (counted as one occurrence).

5. Consecutive TIE's, 2 occurrences for two decisions: TIE 1 and 2, and TIE 9 and 10.

6. First and Last TIE's: TIE 14, the last hand of the Shoe.

7. Early and Late TIE's, TIE's that occur in the first six or last six hands of the Shoe. There were four occurrences for 4 decisions, TIE decisions 1, 2, 3, and 14.

The Adjusted Total Opportunities of 60 is simply a deduction of the opportunities that were counted more than once in classifications 4, 5 and 7. The 7 opportunities outlined in classification number 4 were all duplicated in other classifications, therefore I reduced them to zero for the adjusted total. One duplicate opportunity in classification number 5 was eliminated bringing the adjusted total to one. Duplicates in number seven were reduced to one. The total number of adjustments made was eleven, making the total number of opportunities 60.

These adjustments were made for clarity. There will always be some duplication or overlap among pattern classifications. This is fine because if you miss one pattern and its associated Bet Selection Method, you may pick it up anyway with another. This is of course very helpful.

60 adjusted player advantages out of the 80 total decisions is a great Shoe. However, a word of caution, this number of opportunities is at the high-end of the scale. Typically you will get Shoes that have more in the range of 26 to 40 good opportunities, about 54 % of the time.

Table 9 is a summary of the consecutive win streak opportunities. This Shoe had four excellent consecutive winning streaks. The best was a pair of matching streaks of eight wins each, BANK wins 6 to 13, immediately followed by PLAYER wins 6 to 13.

Notice I won BANK decisions 6 and 7, but lost 8. The reason for this is that I was looking for a repeat pattern of two wins on the PLAYER side. But having lost 8, I immediately switched over to BANK and stayed on BANK for the next 8 decisions.

Consecutive Winning Streak Summary

CONSECUTIVE WIN SEQUENCES	BANK OCCURRENCES	PLAYER OCCURENCES	TOTAL OCCURRENCES	TOTAL # OF HANDS
1	9	8	17	17
2	3	4	7	14
3	1	1	2	6
4	0	0	0	0
5	0	0	0	0
6	0	1	1	6
7	1	0	1	7
8	1	1	2	16
9 & Up	0	0	0	0
TOTAL HANDS:				66

Table 9

On hand 27 I bet BANK because BANK was on a winning streak. Normally following a TIE I would place my next bet opposite the decision before the TIE. But, when PLAYER won hand 27, I switched to PLAYER looking for a matching win streak of 8 straight. This is why I bet BANK on hand 35 instead of PLAYER; PLAYER already matched the 8 straight BANK win streak.

The other two win streaks of seven by BANK (BANK wins 24 through 30) and six by PLAYER (PLAYER wins 28 through 33) were still great even though I missed three of the 13 wins.

These four win streaks, totaling 29 decisions (of which I won 24), accounted for 48% of the 60 total adjusted opportunities.

Summary

If you carefully review the practice score-card just completed, and study the individual betting cards for this Shoe, you should have a pretty good idea how I play the game of Baccarat. It may not be, as easy as you first thought, but if you follow an organized game plan, and apply the techniques, you can become a good player in a fairly short period of time. So continue to practice and practice, it is the best way to learn and improve. There are no shortcuts.

22 - 75-Day Practice Plan

Another question I am frequently asked is how one can become a good Baccarat player. Answer: knowledge, practice, experience, mental toughness, a game plan, plus a keen desire to win. All six ingredients are necessary. An old proverb and a favorite of mine says it well.

> *"Knowledge without wisdom is like a load of books on the back of an ass."*

The wisdom is acquired through practice and the application of practiced-skills during actual Casino play.

Surprisingly, one can become a fairly good Baccarat player in a relatively short period of time. This is because the game is so simple to play. There are no draw-decisions to be made by the player as the cards are dealt. The automatic rules of play govern how the deal proceeds. Therefore, the player does not have to learn any strategies about drawing additional cards or counting. The player need only devote their full attention and concentration to learning and reading the patterns and trends, and selecting the corresponding wagering strategy.

In the past, the problem was the lack of any good published information on the fine points of playing Baccarat.

My first book, *POWER BACCARAT*, and my column in *GAMING TODAY* have helped, I hope, to fill this void. *POWER BACCARAT 2*, provides the instructions needed to become a very good, and ultimately an expert player.

But, just getting the information is not enough. One has to dedicate the time and make the effort studying and practicing the methods and techniques necessary to skillfully play the game. There are still no shortcuts!

How much time and effort will it take? Not really as much as one would think. Completing the 75-day practice-plan outlined here should make you a pretty good player, probably better than two-thirds of the Baccarat players I see. With continued study and practice, and a good bit more experience, one can rise to the top of the class, perhaps within the top 10 to 15% of all players. At this level, along with the required mental toughness, you should be a very successful player. First, lets get you into the top 40%. After that, it is all up to you!

Power Baccarat 2 Practice Scorecard

The practice scorecard in Figure 20 is an excellent practice tool. Copy it, blow it up to increase its size, and use it to practice. You can also write to me to obtain a full-size copy. Simply send a self addressed envelop or provide your e-mail address.

The practice scorecard has several very good features. It combines a scorecard for recording the results of each decision (up to 84 hands) with a wagering record for tracking the bets you make and the cumulative results.

For the *List Bet $* column, note the bet(s) amounts to be made for each hand. For example, 15/5 means $15 on the BANK or PLAYER, and $5 on the TIE. In the next column, circle the bet(s) you make corresponding to the dollar amounts written in the first column.

The next column provides space to keep track of the cumulative results. In the example, suppose the bets 15/5 are $15 on the BANK and $5 on the TIE. BANK wins, resulting in a cumulative win of +10, which would be so recorded in the column *Cumul. $ Win/Loss*. A $15 win on the BANK and a loss of $5 on the TIE, produces a win of $10. If PLAYER won the hand, the loss would be recorded as minus 15 (the $10 BANK and $5 TIE bets both lost). Proceed on this basis practice hand by practice hand. It is not necessary to account for any commissions in practice.

In the next two columns, record the score just as you would on a scorecard completed during actual play. In the example, write the number 1 and circle it under the *BK* column signifying that BANK won the hand, it was the first win for the BANK and you won the bet. Always use the same scoring technique in practice that you intend to use in actual Casino play.

When the practice Shoe is done, prepare a statistical summary like the one I completed for the Shoe I played-out in the last Chapter. Spend some time carefully studying the scorecard. It is important to review how well the Shoe was played, and it is necessary to identify any areas that require improvement.

HD #	HD #	List Bet $	Circle Bets For	Cumul. $ Win/Loss	Score BK	PL
1	43		B/P/T			
2	44		B/P/T			
3	45		B/P/T			
4	46		B/P/T			
5	47		B/P/T			
6	48		B/P/T			
7	49		B/P/T			
8	50		B/P/T			
9	51		B/P/T			
10	52		B/P/T			
11	53		B/P/T			
12	54		B/P/T			
13	55		B/P/T			
14	56		B/P/T			
15	57		B/P/T			
16	58		B/P/T			
17	59		B/P/T			
18	60		B/P/T			
19	61		B/P/T			
20	62		B/P/T			
21	63		B/P/T			
22	64		B/P/T			
23	65		B/P/T			
24	66		B/P/T			
25	67		B/P/T			
26	68		B/P/T			
27	69		B/P/T			
28	70		B/P/T			
29	71		B/P/T			
30	72		B/P/T			
31	73		B/P/T			
32	74		B/P/T			
33	75		B/P/T			
34	76		B/P/T			
35	77		B/P/T			
36	78		B/P/T			
37	79		B/P/T			
38	80		B/P/T			
39	81		B/P/T			
40	82		B/P/T			
41	83		B/P/T			
42	84		B/P/T			

Figure 20

75-Day Practice Plan

1. Carefully read and study the book. Read the entire book through first, then go back and read it again more carefully. Use a highlighter to identify the key techniques and strategies you want to go back to.
   Time: 10 Days
2. Obtain eight decks of regular playing cards and discard the jokers. Deal a few hundred hands to get a feel for the game. Follow the proper shuffling procedures so that your practice play is dealt the same way as it would be in the Casino.
   Time: 5 Days
3. Play many practice hands using a practice scorecard like the one in this book. Record the results of each hand on the scorecard. Use the scoring technique covered in the book. The scorecard also contains space to indicate wagers, cumulative won/loss statistics and the outcomes of the hands. After each practice Shoe, study completed scorecards and notice the patterns and trends. Make notes on the cards indicating the patterns that you did not recognize or missed.
   Time: 30 Days
4. Continue as in three above, but in this phase apply the bet selection and bet progression techniques to your play. Repeat this process over and over again progressively increasing the speed in which you are able to complete the decision-making process. You should play at least 30 complete Baccarat Shoes.
   Time: 30 Days

Finally get to a Casino and test your newly
acquired skills in the heat-of-the-action.
Play at a table that offers the lowest minimum bet, preferably $5 or less. Play no more
than two Shoes at a sitting unless you are
really hot.

One day in the practice plan is approximately
2 hours. After about 150 hours of practice,
study and play, you will indeed be a very
good Baccarat player, in the top 40!

SECTION V

ODDS & ENDS

23 - Making A Living

Can you make a living playing Baccarat? The answer is a qualified yes. It must be qualified because very few players have the required skills, and fewer yet have the burning desire to quit their jobs and play for a living. But, anyone with sufficient motivation and dedication can become good enough to make a living playing Baccarat.

Baccarat, along with Sports Wagering and Poker, would be the three most logical choices if one wanted to make a living as a professional gambler. Baccarat would be the best choice of the three. However, the game then becomes your livelihood, not a recreational pursuit; a transition that is possible, but extremely difficult. When the vast majority of recreational players don't even take the time to become somewhat competent, it is difficult to imagine anyone making the commitment required to become a professional.

Anyone considering such a radical career change should first become an expert player, then put together a sufficient bankroll, and start a transition period of part-time play (while employed) to gauge the potential for success. This transition period must be long enough to become absolutely convinced that one could indeed make a good living playing the game.

A reasonable transition period would be six months to a year, depending how often one can play in a Casino. If you do not live nearby a major Casino location it will require more time, perhaps as much as three years.

Ideally, one must make enough money during this transition period to project potential earnings after switching to full-time play. Remember, once you decide to go full-time, there will be a lot more pressure to win. Baccarat is not a get-rich-quick proposition.

Instead, become an expert player (this will take a few years), keep your job, and supplement your income playing Baccarat. The better you get, the more you will win, and the more often you can make trips to the various vacation spots that offer the game. Of course, the more you play and the higher you bet, the more comps you will receive. Some of these trips will of course be free! Maintaining an amateur status has a lot less pressure, and it will be a lot more fun.

Buy the Video and Get Rich!

There are several hucksters in the market place publicizing the notion that anyone can become rich (very rich by anyone's standards) playing Baccarat. Simply pay a few hundred dollars for their videotapes and instruction manuals, and you can make hundreds of thousands of dollars annually. This and other get-rich-quick gambling promotions are pipedreams. The hucksters are the only ones getting rich. If there is one lesson everyone should know by now, in life, few riches come without working hard.

If it sounds too good to be true, it's a rip-off! Save your money and don't be fooled by these get-rich-quick ads. W. C. Fields said, "*A sucker is born every day.*" Don't be one of them!

24 - Small Bankrolls & Experts

Even with a small bankroll you can play the great game of Baccarat. Las Vegas is the best place to play, and you can find a lot of low-minimum-bet games. $5 dollar minimums are very easy to find. You can also find Casinos that charge 4% commission instead of the usual 5%. These are the kinds of games the small bankroll player must look for.

It is also best to find a game with only two or three other players, and week-day play is best. Your strategy will be to Hit'em and Run. That is, bet only when a good opportunity comes along. Unlike Blackjack where a wager must be made on every hand, in Baccarat it is not uncommon to sit-out a few hands from time to time. However, in crowded conditions with players waiting for seats, the Casino may frown upon this strategy, particularly when sitting-out for several successive decisions repeatedly.

Begin play at the start of a new Shoe, unless the Shoe in-play is a good one. By this I mean that either or both PLAYER and BANK wins are frequently long (4 or more consecutive decisions), then get-in and follow the decision pattern. To determine if there is a good opportunity, check the scorecard of one of the other players. A winning player will usually be happy to show his or her card.

Assume you start play at the beginning of the Shoe. An average Shoe will contain 80 decisions, seven of which will be TIE's. There will be at least 20 good opportunities, your best profit-makers.

The Bankroll for the Shoe will be $150. The objective will be to at least double it. Use a Stop-Loss Point of $75 (quit if you lose half your Stake of $150), and the win goals are $50, $75, $100 and so on. You will quit before you fall back below any win goal achieved. For example, if you win $75 quit before falling back below the last win goal of $50.

The strategy will be to bet only when a favorable opportunity occurs according to your analysis of the existing trends and patterns as the game plays-out. These opportunities will be winning streaks of three or more straight decisions, and any repetitive patterns, including TIE's. At the start of the Shoe do not bet. Wait until you get a feel for how the game is going. This may take several or more decisions. Be patient, and record the outcomes on your scorecard.

Many Casinos will continue to deal a few hands even when no one is betting. This is a very important advantage. Make the most of it if you are the only player, and do not want to make a bet. Simply tell the Dealer *No bet*, and ask him or her to deal a few hands.

Study your scorecard and look for patterns, especially those involving TIE's, which are more prevalent when there are more than the usual seven TIE decisions. Remember a TIE-bet win pays 8 to 1!

The pattern to watch for is multiple TIE decisions with only a few decisions (1 to 4) between them; the TIE's occur in bunches. Bet $1 on the first attempt, and raise your bets to $2, $4 and so on following any wins.

Make your first bet when an opportunity occurs. Use a few basic bet progressions to size your bets. When you win the first bet in any series, go ahead with the next and so on. But, stop the series if you lose any bet within the series. Start over with the same series, or select another bet progression.

You do not have to be a high-roller to play Mini-Baccarat. A small Stake will do just fine with a carefully formulated plan, and enough practice to perfect it.

You Do Not Have To Be an Expert To Win!

There is only one Casino game that can be consistently beat without being an expert player, and that game is Baccarat. Blackjack, Craps and Poker require a substantially higher degree of playing skill (as well as a larger bankroll). But, disregarding the need for a larger bankroll, very few players have the necessary skills, and fewer still take the time and effort needed to acquire such skills.

The need for a relatively larger bankroll, and the requirement to be essentially an expert player are two of the best reasons NOT to play Blackjack, Craps or Poker. They are also very good reasons to play Baccarat instead. Baccarat is a game of streaks and patterns in the decision outcomes, perhaps the best reason to play the game.

These opportunities offer a reasonably
skilled player an advantage over the Casino.
Reasonably skilled means having a good knowledge of the types of streaks and patterns
that are typical in the outcomes of the decisions. A player that is familiar with the
kinds of outcomes that produce these advantages will be a consistent winner if he or
she applies a Hit'em and Run strategy.

It is a fairly easy proposition to acquire a
good knowledge base of the common types of
streaks and patterns in the outcomes. But it
is a little more difficult developing and applying a consistent play strategy, one that
is disciplined and carefully managed. This
latter requirement is needed for winning play
in any Casino game one chooses to play.
Therefore, this being essentially equal to a
great degree for all games, the skill needed
to play Baccarat is much easier to acquire.

If a beginner were to choose a Casino game to
concentrate on, Baccarat should be on the top
of the list. A reasonable number of hours of
study and practice, plus a few more hours of
play will provide the basics. After several
more days of study and practice (as little as
20 hours), any beginner can become a fairly
good player.

Baccarat can be played for as little as $5
dollars a hand and you do not have to play
every decision. A good player will be patient
and wait for the best opportunities, then
make a bet(s). This is what I refer to as the
Hit'em and Run play strategy. Look for the
best opportunities, then make your move, aggressive and decisive. If there are no opportunities, do not bet. Patience is a very important part of the strategy.

Waiting for the best opportunities will conserve your bankroll leaving you flush to take
full advantage when one comes along.

Being an expert Baccarat player will certainly be more rewarding, but one does not
have to be an expert, or even a highly
skilled player to consistently beat the game.
Put in some study time and effort, and give
Baccarat a serious try. You probably cannot
do any worse than you are now playing those
other Casino games, but then again, you may
do a whole lot better playing Baccarat - the
best Casino game!

25 - Luck, Intuition And ESP

In any games of chance, you will often hear these words: Luck, Intuition and Extra-Sensory-Perception (ESP), particularly the word luck. But, do they really have a role in the game of Baccarat?

The dictionary definition of luck is: *a force that brings good fortune; favoring chance.* Because Baccarat is a game of frequent streaks and patterns, players often associate a losing streak with bad luck, or a winning streak with good luck. The fact is that these frequent streaks and patterns are what make the game of Baccarat the best Casino game to play. But, because the average player is inexperienced, these streaks seem to defy chance. The patterns are seldom recognized without sufficient training, and are viewed as lucky. The average player often bets against them, rather than going-with-the-flow (one of the golden rules of Baccarat). As a result, the average player can have some very bad losing streaks, their translation: *Bad Luck!*

This is, of course, an extremely erroneous conclusion. Their losses have nothing to do with bad luck. They are simply due to ignorance. All it takes to overcome their *Bad Luck* is a little knowledge and experience.

My own opinion about luck is best expressed in the words of Emerson:

On the other hand, when a player is winning, and most importantly, winning consistently, most everyone will say it is due to good luck.

> *"Shallow men believe in luck, believe in circumstances: it was somebody's name, or he happened to be there at the time, or it was so then, and another day it would have been otherwise. Strong men believe in cause and effect."*

Quite the contrary, a Baccarat player wins consistently when he or she is experienced, and follows a highly disciplined approach. Good luck has nothing to do with it!

What about intuition? The dictionary definition is: *the power or faculty of attaining direct knowledge or cognition without rational thought and inference; quick and ready insight.* Intuition is an entirely different matter; it presupposes that one has some built-in skills to better comprehend. Intuition exerts an internal influence rather than the external influences associated with luck.

In Baccarat, intuition is actually the power to quickly read the trends and patterns in the outcomes. The ability to gain a ready insight simply by keeping an organized Baccarat scorecard. In other words, it is a skill acquired only through long hours of practice and study, together with years of actual Casino play. Intuition is a skill only the most expert Baccarat players possess.

Finally, what about Extra-Sensory-Perception or ESP? Applying the notion of ESP to Baccarat, in its purest form, would be the ability to predict the outcomes of the decisions with little or no knowledge about the game itself. The key phrase: *with little or knowledge about the game itself.* That is, ESP is a power one is born with, not a skill that can be acquired.

In summary, luck cannot be relied upon to win. Intuition is a skill only the best players have, and ESP is a natural ability (an ability that would certainly be an advantage, for gaming purposes anyway). If one is serious about becoming an expert player, there is no substitute for knowledge and experience. Luck and ESP simply are not relevant!

26 - In The Zone

One of my first personal experiences with the game of Baccarat was a winning streak for BANK of 12 straight wins. This streak produced my largest single gaming profit. Subsequent forays convinced me that Baccarat provided a relatively large number of winning opportunities; a very attractive reason to play, and one that makes it the best Casino game.

Over the years my playing skills improved, and I found I was able to identify winning opportunities before they happened. By keeping a scorecard and watching for repetitive patterns, it was often possible to predict future outcomes of the decisions. This was an extremely important revelation. However, this process was by no means an exact science. Sometimes what I thought would occur did not. But, more often than not, the opportunities that looked probable did in fact occur.

I was winning on a regular basis, but not as much as would be indicated by the number of winning decisions. I spent many hours studying and practicing, largely by trial and error. Eventually, I created an improved scoring method, developed new techniques and strategies, and put together a disciplined game plan.

Additionally, I identified and classified the most common and profitable Baccarat patterns. TIE patterns were also identified and classified for the first time, and published in my first book. The realization that TIE's often occur in repetitive patterns, and often with very few hands between them, particularly in TIE-RICH Shoes (Shoes that contain an average of 11 TIE's), proved to be very profitable.

But, because there was so little technical information about the game, this learning process took several years. Now, any player serious enough to want to improve his or her game can simply practice and study the *POWER BACCARAT* methods as a blueprint. One can become a good player in a few months, and quite advanced in a year or so with enough actual Casino play. Reaching the next level however is not something that can be taught. At the expert level, both instinct and intuition are applied. These skills can only be developed and sharpened with a great deal of actual play experience.

If you are extremely good at something, chances are that you apply instinct and intuition to produce a positive result (whether you know it or not). I compare the application of instinct and intuition to athletes who are *IN-THE-ZONE*. For example, the running-back who seems to glide effortlessly down the field cutting through, and bouncing off would-be tacklers, or the shooting-guard who cannot seem to miss a shot. Even though there is extreme physical or mental exertion, a person *IN-THE-ZONE* is calm, sees the entire field of action, and yet is very focused.

When I am *IN-THE-ZONE* playing Baccarat, I believe I can win every hand. My scorecard almost talks to me, and my wagering decisions are quick and decisive; there is no thinking, no hesitation. My *IN-THE-ZONE* scorecards are always big wins. Unfortunately I am not always *IN-THE-ZONE*.

You can benefit from *IN-THE-ZONE* players too. If you find yourself in a game of Baccarat and another player cannot seem to lose, follow their lead. Wait for him or her to bet, and bet exactly the same way. When she bets BANK and TIE, you must also bet BANK and TIE.

In team play the hot-hand gets the ball; Isiah Thomas, the great guard for the Pistons, referred to it as *feed the pig*. If you become good enough to occasionally play Baccarat *IN-THE-ZONE* notice how many players will wait to see how you bet before they do!

27 - New Twists, Or Just Nonsense?

Because Baccarat is a big-money game, there are always those who are looking for some new twist that can be employed to beat the game. Two of my *favorites* are counting and wagering on both BANK and PLAYER simultaneously.

Card Counting

The counting theory in Baccarat, like Blackjack, provides a method for identifying potential advantages based on the remaining mix of the cards. The count will determine when the remaining mix of cards favors one bet over the other (BANK over PLAYER, or vice versa). The count starts by favoring BANK since the rules of the game give the BANK hand a slight edge. From there, a continued positive count favors BANK, and a negative one favors PLAYER.

Unlike Blackjack, Baccarat card counting does not provide a significant statistical edge. According to Dr. Thorpe, who published the famous counting strategy for Blackjack, the only real opportunities that can be identified by counting cards in Baccarat occur in the last 5 to 20 <u>cards</u> of the 8-deck Shoe. This is only one hand, or at most, six hands. Dr. Thorpe therefore correctly concluded, that Baccarat card-counting strategies are not productive.

In fact, the effort needed to count an 8-deck Shoe is simply not justified for the slight advantage one might obtain at the very end of the Shoe. Counting cards is a complete waste of time. The level of concentration required to perform any Baccarat counting strategy would be much better applied to evaluating potential patterns in the outcomes, the real advantages in the game. Remember that an average Baccarat Shoe will contain at least 20 good opportunities, many more than any counting strategy could identify.

Wagering On Both BANK and PLAYER

A second twist, and perhaps the silliest I have seen, is wagering both ways. That is, betting on both the BANK and PLAYER at the same time, but in unequal amounts. Using this strategy, a player would bet, for example, $10 on the BANK and $15 on PLAYER for the same hand. Of course the obvious question is why not simply bet the $5 difference on PLAYER. Sometimes the obvious is not so obvious!

This strategy is also more costly when the higher wager is bet on the BANK hand. For a bet of $100 on the BANK and $50 on PLAYER, the net gain for a BANK win is $50, less the $5 commission on the winning $100 BANK bet. If instead, one simply bet $50 on the BANK, the commission would be only $2.50. The extra commission cost can add-up quickly when making larger bets on the BANK. The overall affect is giving-up any gains afforded from the low Casino advantage.

I have played with individuals using this ridiculous wagering technique and can only politely conclude they must be quite misguided.

They are also forced to endure the incredulous looks and comments from the other players and Dealers. In fairness to the Baccarat players who are women, I have never seen a woman play the game in this manner.

If you want to win playing Baccarat, stick to the basics. Look for those pattern opportunities, and bet on them. The funny little twists are just nonsense, and that's a fact!

Baccarat on the Internet

Casinos on the Internet account for hundreds of millions of dollars in additional gaming revenues. Access the World Wide Web, select an Internet Casino, download and install the free software, register with them and open an account, and you are gambling in the comfort of your home. It is a very simple process. But beware, some downloads may take some time, anywhere from ten to thirty minutes depending on the speed of your modem. You will also need at least 16mg of RAM.

Once the software is downloaded on your PC, simply log-on to the Net and click-on the icon or file name on your PC (the software previously downloaded) representing the Casino, and enter your password. The Casino will be contacted automatically.

Most Internet Casinos will also let you play for free before playing for real money. The best ones encourage you to play for free first so you can become familiar with the games and all of the gaming procedures.

You should also know that the United States and many state governments consider gaming on Internet Casinos to be illegal. This is why nearly all of the Internet Casinos are located outside of the United States. A large number of them operate out of the Caribbean, and some even as far away as Australia. Typically Internet Casinos are licensed by the country within which they operate.

There is little the Federal or State governments can do to enforce the statutes as currently written. The future is however uncertain. New laws prohibiting Internet gambling will continue to be introduced, likely targeting service providers such as the financial institutions and the Internet Service Providers. But, the opposition to such laws would be very great, and I personally give them no chance of passage.

There are several dozen Internet Casinos to choose from. The types of games offered, the rules of the games, gaming visual affects, and customer support vary widely. Many do not offer Baccarat. And of those that do offer Baccarat, I have not found one Internet Casino that plays the game the way it should be played. The rules of Baccarat are the same, but the game itself is not set-up the same way that it would be in an actual Casino.

What I mean by this is that in a real Casino, eight decks of cards would be shuffled and cut. All 416 cards are now fixed and ready to be dealt from the Shoe. They will only be re-shuffled after all the cards in the eight decks are dealt. Playing Baccarat on the Internet is completely different. Internet Casinos typically use one deck of cards and re-shuffle after each and every hand.

Therefore, the player cannot practice according to the Power Baccarat methods I advocate. The trends and patterns one has to be familiar with to become a good player will not play-out in the same manner as they would with a fixed eight deck Shoe.

The only real use in playing Baccarat on the Internet is to get a feel for the game in a more Casino-like environment. You can certainly have a little fun playing and get used to the rules, but that is about all. The bottom line: thumbs down to both serious practice and playing Baccarat for money on the Internet. Save it for an actual Casino vacation.

No-Commission Baccarat

A new version of Baccarat was recently introduced in Las Vegas at Bally's and the Hilton. It is called No-commission Baccarat; no commission is charged on winning BANK wagers.

The modified rules of the no-commission game give the Casino its edge without charging a commission. Both PLAYER and BANK hands stand on totals of six and higher, and draw a third card on totals of five or less. There is no draw for either hand when one hand has a natural (a two-card total of 8 or 9). In addition, a winning total of three by either the BANK or PLAYER is a push; the opposite hand losses. For example, if you bet BANK and BANK wins with a total of three, it is a push. If you bet PLAYER and BANK wins with a total of three, of course you lose. TIE hands pay 9 to 1 instead of 8 to 1, and you can also make a side-bet that the next hand will be a natural; it pays 3 to 2. However, the natural side-bet should be avoided.

The game is currently played at a mini-Baccarat-size table. It features bar-coded cards, electronic scoring and an electronic scoreboard. As the cards are dealt from the Shoe (by the Dealer), they are passed under a bar-code reader. The reader then displays the card-count on the computer screen, and the result of the decision on the electronic scorecard. The colorful display shows the scorecard, and the number of hands won by BANK, PLAYER and the number of TIE's. As with any bar-code device, more than one pass of the cards through the reader may be necessary to register the card-count. During my recent trials of the game this was a fairly common occurrence.

Baccarat is one of the few existing Casino table games that has essentially remained unchanged for many years. The new modified version, No-commission Baccarat, was apparently designed to appeal to those customers who wrongly perceive the traditional game to have a higher Casino advantage and harder to beat (with its 5% commission and more complex BANK hand third-card draw rules). Thus, players who have not played Baccarat may find No-commission Baccarat appealing.

However, regular Baccarat players will find No-commission Baccarat far less appealing. First, regular Baccarat players have no problem with the draw rules. Second, the higher Casino advantage for the no-commission game makes regular Baccarat a better play. Therefore, there is no reason for a regular Baccarat player to switch to the no-commission version of the game.

For the Casino, the no-commission game gives them a higher advantage, and is somewhat faster so it produces more decisions per hour (because the Dealer does not have to account for and accumulate commissions). It also has the possibility of attracting new Baccarat customers (customers who have never played Baccarat, or just tried the traditional game a few times and found it difficult). For the no-commission game to last, the Casino will have to attract a significant number of new customers. I personally do not give this much of a chance.

The No-commission Baccarat innovation that could be applied to traditional Baccarat is the electronic scoring and computerized display. Computerization should also appeal to new customers.

The bottom line: New Baccarat players may give No-commission Baccarat a try, but, for regular Baccarat players, the no-commission version is simply not attractive.

28 - Baccarat Myths

I have addressed the advantages of playing Baccarat over Craps and Blackjack in the first Chapter of this book. Even though Baccarat has many advantages, the facts do not always hold-up against some of the widely held myths, and common misconceptions many Casino patrons have about the game.

Casino Advantage

The first and most often heard myth, concerns the commission charged to any player winning a bet on BANK. The typical player reasons that the Casino advantage is the same as the commission charged, so why play Baccarat when they could play Craps or Blackjack and pay no commission. Of course this is just nonsense; Chapter 6 provides a complete description of the mathematics involved. I am referring to this again here because the Casino advantage for Baccarat is so misunderstood.

The Casino advantage for Craps is 1.41% on the PASS LINE, and 1.40% on the DON'T PASS LINE.

For Blackjack, the Casino advantage varies according to the rules allowed (Surrender be-ing the most important rule for the player, followed by Doubling-Down and Splitting on any cards and pairs, and so on) and the abil-ity and skill of the player.

The average Blackjack player faces a Casino advantage of at least 5%, and without favorable rules, the advantage to the Casino is much higher.

The Casino advantage for Baccarat on BANK wagers is 1.06%, and on PLAYER wagers 1.23%; both are far less than 5%, and even less than the Casino advantage for Craps. The next time you hear the Casino advantage for Baccarat is 5%, set them straight. They still probably won't believe you!

Bet BANK, It Wins More Often, OR Bet PLAYER Because No Commission Is Charged

There are two other related misconceptions about the game of Baccarat. Bet on BANK because it wins more often, and the contrary view, bet PLAYER because there is no commission on winning PLAYER wagers. In the first place, you have already seen the very slight difference between BANK and PLAYER Casino advantage. Over the long run, 45.84% of the time BANK wins, and 44.61% of the time PLAYER wins. The difference is only 0.17% (1.23% less 1.06%), hardly a basis for any betting methodology.

In the short-run anything can happen; individual Shoes can be dominated by the BANK or the PLAYER. I have played Shoes where PLAYER won 80% of the hands and vice-versa. Baccarat is a game of streaks and patterns, and *Going-With-the-Flow* is the first and foremost rule.

A systematic methodology of betting only on BANK or PLAYER, for the corresponding flow or trend, would be a reasonable approach. But, blindly betting on one, or the other, based on the acceptance of the aforementioned misconceptions is plain ridiculous. Yet, this is exactly how some players play the game.

Cost-to-Play?

With the rising popularity of Baccarat, particularly Mini-Baccarat, it is not surprising to read more and more about the game. Recent articles have described the huge increase in the Mini-Baccarat drop. Gaming Today reported that since 1993 the drop in downtown Las Vegas went from less than $8 million to some $37 million. Mini-Baccarat is the fifth largest table game in both drop and win. With the action heating-up, more and more players are giving the game a serious try. At the same time, fewer and fewer players are playing Blackjack; thankfully this trend will continue.

Of course with its newfound popularity, articles describing the game of Mini-Baccarat have also mushroomed. Unfortunately, many do a disservice to the reader. Case-in-point, a recent multiple-page article on the game is typical. Ninety-five percent of the article was devoted to describing the rules and offering a few comparative facts. The few remaining paragraphs describe something called the *cost to play*, and a suggested play strategy. Both were completely useless.

The article describes in some detail what is referred to as ones expected hourly cost, or expected loss for an hour of play. This cost is calculated taking a $5 wager, multiplied by the Casino advantage, times the number of Baccarat hands played in an hour. The resulting figure, a very low dollar number, is meaningless. In fact, it is quite dangerous. First-time players can be mislead into believing that the game can be played for long periods with little risk.

This is of course not true. A player who knows anything about the game never plays every hand, and certainly does not bet the same amount hand after hand, minimum or otherwise.

This cost-to-play nonsense was followed by the equally stupid advice to bet-only-the-BANK. The article completely ignores the single most important reason to play the game: the common streaks and patterns in the outcomes. They are a Baccarat players best opportunities.

New players following this very poor advice will certainly not have favorable experiences. It is unfortunate for the game, and for the players, when some well-known gaming publications carry such articles as bad as the example I cited on Mini-Baccarat. It just goes to show, do not believe everything you read, even from what would appear to be a reliable source. Check the facts for yourself and get second opinions, particularly dissenting ones that challenge conventional thinking.

Lesson Learned: be skeptical of what you read, especially when it comes to applying it with real money. Baccarat is by far the best Casino game; unfortunately, not all published articles do it justice!

29 - All Shoes Are Not Equal

Essentially my advice on playing the game of Baccarat boils down to developing and practice-perfecting a consistent disciplined approach, using a Hit'em and Run strategy. As such, the Casinos you choose to play at should also have standard methods and consistent procedures for dealing the game. This is important because any variation from the standard can have a negative effect, particularly during favorable opportunities.

So just what are the standard methods and procedures for dealing the game? It is necessary for you to understand them so you can immediately recognize any deviation. For example, suppose you are playing Poker, the Dealer offers you the cards to make the cut, you cut them, and the Dealer begins to deal. But, you notice that the Dealer is dealing them from the bottom of the deck! This would indeed be a significant deviation from a normal deal. I suspect you would not play under such circumstances. The same notion applies to the game of Baccarat; any deviation from the normal methods should be cause for choosing not to play at that Casino.

In Baccarat there is a standard procedure for making ready the cards for the game. Some Casinos shuffle them by hand; others use a shuffling machine. Both methods are fine.

At the end of the shuffle, and during the deal, is when you must pay close attention to the procedures. There are two major deviations I have seen, all at the Mini-Baccarat tables.

Cutting the Cards

One of the deviations occurs after the cut of the cards by one of the players. Using proper procedures, after the cut the Dealer will remove a number of cards from the back of the deck (remember the deck in Baccarat actually means eight decks put together). Starting from the last card of the deck, the Dealer then counts out fourteen cards and inserts the colored marker-card. When this card appears toward the end of the Shoe, it is the signal that only one more hand is left to play.

The improper method used by some Casinos is removing the cards from the front of the deck (after the cut) to count out fourteen. They then place them at the back of the Shoe. I find this disconcerting, especially when I was the one who cut the cards (even though after the cut all Casinos burn a few cards prior to the start of the deal).

Card-Burns

The second deviation is my personal all-time *favorite*. Some Casinos burn a card every time the relief Dealer takes-over. I find this procedure unacceptable, and it is often done almost surreptitiously, as though the Casino doesn't want players to notice that they are trying to change the complexion of the Shoe.

It is also more frequently done when the Casino has been paying-out a lot of money. Then they then change Dealers more often.

Any way you slice it, I do not appreciate surprises in the manner I am accustomed to seeing the game of Baccarat dealt. When I observe card preparation and dealing deviations, I take my business elsewhere. You should too!

30 - Comps, Tips, Etc.

Everyone believes they are entitled to comps (short for complimentary) or freebies Casinos usually reserve for preferred players.

Comps were originally offered by the Casinos to attract high-rollers. With the advent of personal computers, specialized software, and systematic procedures for recording and rating play, comps are now available to all qualified players.

> "The great trouble today is that there are too many people looking for someone to do something for them."
>
> Henry Ford

Casinos give over $1,000,000,000 in comps annually. The combined Drop (money bet on the table games) and Handle (money bet on slots) is over twenty five times greater; that's $25 billion. Comps represent less than 5% of this total. The total table game hold (win divided by the drop) is somewhere in the neighborhood of 15 percent. Casinos give back comps worth only about 2 to 5 cents on the dollar.

Generally, a mathematical calculation, using the following factors, will be used to determine if a player qualifies for comps:

1. The Casino game played. The Casino advantage varies between games, and among the available bets.
2. Duration of play.
3. Average bet size.
4. Player's skill level.
5. Players style; loose, conservative, or aggressive.

These factors are not of equal importance, a weighting factor is applied. Utilizing some, or even all of the above factors, the Casino will calculate a theoretical win figure (the amount of money the Casino should win from the player). The comps that can be given back are based upon a percentage of this win amount, usually somewhere between 15% and 30% of the calculated win figure. To be comped, you will generally have to risk 5-10 times the value the comp.

Duration of play and bet size are the most important factors considered by the Casino. Combined, they represent the amount of money players put into play (in action) over a period of time.

If one bets on average $100 per decision and plays 10 hours in a 24-hour period, this would represent total action of well over $100,000. A regular visitor, who plays at this level, will be putting in action a few million dollars each year. Play at this level should at least get the player free suites, meals, and shows. But one thing should be perfectly clear; you don't get something for nothing!

My own experience supports one other important fact. The Casino wants your business. Competition is tough, and if your Casino is not taking care of you, go elsewhere. Most will make the effort to keep your business, win or lose, with comps for qualified play. The key words: qualified play. But, keep in mind, you play to win, not to get comps!

Having said that, the first step is yours. The Casino doesn't know you from anybody else unless you play, and ask to be rated. To give yourself the best possible opportunity to earn comps, take the following steps:

1. Concentrate play at 2 or 3 Casinos.
2. Obtain a comp (rating) card from these Casinos, and be sure to hand it to the Dealer when you buy-in.
3. Change your entire Stake for that Session into chips so that the Casino will record your buy-in. Do not exchange it a bit at a time.
4. Visit your Casinos during weekdays or off-season periods, comps are easier to obtain.
5. If possible, play at a table where your minimum bet is higher than the table minimum bet. You'll be noticed.
6. If you play with Casino credit (Markers), cash in your chips after a win, and write another Marker when resuming play. It will appear that you are putting more new cash in action. However, if the cashier asks if you have any Markers, pay them off.
7. Be friendly and outgoing. Remember the names of Dealers and Floor Persons, and greet them by name. Get to know the people who serve you, including a Casino Host; make reservations through him/her.
8. If you are not comped a room, ask for the Casino-rate when you check in, it may be 50% lower.

9. Apply for Casino credit. Make inquiries well before your next trip. You will be required to complete a credit application. With Casino credit, you will be able to write a personal check at the end of your visit to pay-off any outstanding Markers. Ensure the checking account you intend to use is specified on the credit application. When you play, simply ask the Dealer for a Marker, and specify the amount (some portion of your credit line).

10. In addition to Casino credit, you can also make cash deposits to your account, and then draw it down as needed, cash first then credit.

11. Casino Junkets may also be worth a look. Ask your Casino Host. Many Junkets require that a minimum amount of front money be deposited with the Casino. Get the facts: how much front money, how much money must be generated in Markers, how long must you play, and how much money you must bet. Then determine what expenses the Casino will be cover. If their requirements exceed your normal level of play, forget them.

Casinos are only interested in how much action you give them; how much you bet over a period of time. They know that given sufficient volume, the Casino edge should take care of itself. Strangely, I see player's pocket chips to hide winnings. This is silly because a big win often gets a player classified as wild, and that normally means more comps. The Casino wants to keep your action, so do not hesitate to ask where you stand. Talk to the Casino Host or Pit Supervisor, often they will give you a dinner or show comp. If you are seeing a show, ask for a line pass, there is no waiting, you can go right to the front. Casino Hosts and Supervisors have some discretion, so don't be shy, ask what they can do, you might be pleasantly surprised.

Shop Casinos, play to win and the comps will come automatically.

The Casino Experience

The American Casino has become the ultimate entertainment complex and not just for adults, but for the entire family as well. Charter flights and travel packages to Las Vegas and Atlantic City are plentiful. Kansas City and Detroit, are also major Casino destinations. Shop around for the best deals.

The excitement of a Casino is almost overwhelming. The lights, buzzers, bells, sounds of coins, and the screams of winning customers are wonderful sounds. The plush decor, bargain meals, free drinks, free lounge shows, headline shows, and a very dedicated staff of people, will almost make you feel like one of the rich and famous.

Unfortunately, it is all designed to make it easier to take your money. The cheapskate who walks into a Casino and immediately becomes a big-shot may soon be broke. The atmosphere is designed to make you comfortable and more willing to spend your money. It is all part of the fun and excitement promoted by the Casino. This environment can hurt you, but it can also be enjoyed when you keep your head.

You will always be treated with respect and in a courteous manner by the Casino staff. Reciprocate in kind and you'll get more of the same in return.

To make your Casino visit an enjoyable one, follow these tips:

1. Obtain a comp card or rating card, at the Casino of your choice, and always present it to the Dealer when you play.
2. Make your headline show reservations in advance. They often sell-out quickly.
3. Arrive properly attired. A suit or dress isn't necessary, but a nice outfit will demonstrate some class, and first impressions are important.
4. Always be courteous and show appreciation to all Casino Personnel. Speak to them by name. They will be wearing name-tags. They will soon know your name too, and greet you by name when they see you.
5. Do not ask for a comp. Ask instead what is required to get them. A Casino Floor Person will make a check of the computer records showing your play, and will be happy to explain how you can qualify.
6. Charge all meals and other Casino expenses to your room. At checkout ask the Casino Host to determine if the Casino can comp some of these expenses, you may be surprised what you get.
7. Be courteous to the other players at your table. You may even make a few friends. Be careful, however, not to disturb another players concentration.
8. Tipping is expected. Only tip for courteous services rendered. If you have a complaint, don't hesitate to voice it to the appropriate person. But, do it in a respectful manner. No one likes a loudmouth.

Tipping

Tip for services rendered. The size of any tip should vary based upon how well services were delivered. At a restaurant, 15 to 20% is

the standard <u>if</u> the expected level of service
is delivered. Extraordinary service is rewarded with a larger tip. Sub-standard service is not rewarded.

When I gamble and win, I tip the Dealers provided they have been friendly and helpful.
The worst and rudest Dealers always seem to
be at the Craps table.

A helpful Dealer is one who gives me extra
time to place my bets. Dealers will often
take care of you if you tip. If you don't
have a bet down they may ask if you want to
bet or not. Just asking the question gives an
extra few moments to make a decision.

Dealers are generally paid a minimum wage.
The money received in tips is what makes it a
decent living. Typically, tips are split
among all the Dealers on a shift, either for
all games, or for a specific section of the
Casino.

When tipping a Dealer, put the tip in-action,
make a bet for them. Don't tip like you are
tipping a waiter in a restaurant. Place the
tip as a bet next to your own bet on PLAYER,
or BANK, or TIE, or even both. Then with
their tip riding on the outcome, they obviously will be pulling for a win! If you win,
they win.

If you bet a tip on BANK for the Dealers and
win, no commission is charged on the tip.
Never bet a tip against your own hand. A tip
is always bet along with your own wager. The
more I win, the more I tip. A tip can be for
any amount, including an amount below the table minimum.

Dealers usually work twenty minutes on, twenty off. When the Dealers relief arrives, the Dealer will usually express his thanks to the tipper. He/she may say something like *thank you for the action*, or other such phrase. The new Dealer, having got the *message*, will continue to watch out for you as well.

A helpful Dealer can make you a lot more money than the tips you make as bets for them. They may not cheat for you, but they'll certainly give you the benefit of the doubt on any payoff or commission error.

How much should you tip and when? I will not tip until I exceed my first win goal. After that, I will tip every few hands if I continue to win. As my winnings build, I'll increase the size of my tips, or their frequency.

If you are a $5 to $10 dollar player, tips of $1 are normal. Always bet the tip. If you are winning TIE's, bet a tip for the Dealers on the TIE too! I'll often bet TIE for the Dealers on all 4 to 6 hands of a bunched TIE bet progression when I've been hitting them. It really gets them in the game!

Table Etiquette

Baccarat players are typically a fairly quiet bunch. You won't find the screaming and yelling that is the norm at the Craps table. That's not to say that such behavior is frowned upon at the Baccarat tables, it's just not common. My suggestion is to remain somewhat reserved. In any case, you'll need to concentrate on your play.

You'll find all kinds of players at the Baccarat table just as you will at the other table games. Those that bother me the most have little, if any, consideration for other players. They have no table etiquette, and they are nearly always men. Fortunately however, they remain a minority. Just be prepared for the following types.

The Complainer

The complainer is the guy who blames losing on everything and everybody, except the real reason: poor play. He keeps playing, keeps losing, and keeps complaining. The more he loses, the louder he complains.

When a complainer is at your table, move away from him. Sitting nearby can be quite distracting. I have used such persons to help me bet. I'll wait for him to wager, and bet the opposite. Its surprising how well you can do with his help.

The Big Shot

This is the guy who puts down other players, questions the Dealers, claims to be an expert, brags about big wins he has had at some other Casino, demands comps, and announces tips. He is a loudmouth. When one is in the game, get as far away from him as possible, and quit if you start to lose. They are the worst players to have at any table.

The Helper

The helper is also an expert even though he says he only plays occasionally. He's always telling some other player something about the game, or how to play, and what he says is usually wrong. He will question this, ask why you did that, and will always be quick to point out why you lost. He's a constant interruption to your concentration and therefore a danger. Ask him not to bother you, or move to another seat.

The Teetotaler

The teetotaler is a constant source of irritation not only for you, but for the Dealers as well. They usually know very little about the game, and expect the Dealers to give them a lesson during play. They sit down, produce a twenty-dollar bill, lose it, and pull out another twenty.

The first time he wins on BANK, he immediately wants to pay-down his commission, or perhaps doesn't even know a commission is due. He is constantly interrupting the rhythm of play by occupying the Dealers' time with questions or making small change, and frequently paying-off small commissions. Fortunately you won't find him at the big Baccarat table.

Don't allow any of these kinds of players to distract you. Stay disciplined, maintain your concentration, and focus on your plan. The best advice: have fun, and do unto others, as you would have them do unto you.

31 - References & Order Forms

Additional copies of POWER BACCARAT 2 can be ordered by detaching the order form in this Chapter.

Serious players will also want to obtain additional gaming materials, and subscribe to a good gaming publication. There are two sources that I highly recommend: The **Gamblers Book Club (GBC)** in Las Vegas, and the weekly gaming publication **GAMING TODAY**.

GBC is an excellent source for books and literature on any gaming subject. It is the worlds oldest (since 1964) and largest gaming shop. Call for a copy of the free GBC catalog (1-800-522-1777), or check out their website **www.gamblersbook.com** or stop bye the bookstore at 630 South 11th Street in Las Vegas on your next visit. GBC is open 9 to 5 Monday through Saturday. The telephone number is 702-382-7555. Tell Howard Schwartz I sent you!

GAMING TODAY is the best source for up-to-date gaming information. It is a highly respected publication, and the one the insiders read. It features regular columns on all major gaming subjects, including my column, plus many gaming news items. More information follows at the end of this Chapter. Subscribing is highly recommended.

POWER BACCARAT 2

Order Form

Send **POWER BACCARAT 2** to me at the following address:

Name:_____

Address:_____

_____

City:_____

State / Zip:_____

Enclosed is a Check / Money Order for $22.95
(includes express mail delivery). Additional
copies are $21.00 each; please specify the
number required.

Make payment to Byron Hebert, and mail to:
PO Box 40, Wyandotte, Michigan 48192

Thank You For Your Order

Contact **GAMING TODAY** PO Box 93116, Las Vegas, Nevada, 89193, fax 702-798-2069, E-mail **subscriptions@gamingtoday.com** to subscribe. The rates as of this writing are $135 for six months or $180 for one year. Tell them that I sent you; **GAMING TODAY** for news you can bet on!

32 - Wrap-Up

If you were paid a $10,000 reward if you stopped smoking, maintained a daily exercise routine, or changed your life in some major way, you would probably be quite motivated to do it? But, could you really do it? Maybe. Maybe because if the reward is for something that cannot be accomplished in the short-term it is much harder. And, it is then usually a much greater achievement.

Then again, great achievements are usually made up of many small steps taken one step at a time. By taking them a step at a time, it becomes easier. Setting your sites on a long-term goal, then doing the little things, and taking the little steps that get you there. This takes mental toughness and discipline, very important ingredients for success in life, let alone success in gambling.

Ask yourself how you really achieved something, anything, in your life and you'll likely conclude that you wanted it badly, and did what it took to get it. There were no shortcuts. You had to work for it.

The first step was setting the goal. Next was doing the things you needed to do to reach your goal, and staying with it.

In Casino gaming, you must want to win badly, you must have a plan for doing it, and you must have the discipline to stick to the plan.

If you play in a Casino twice a year and lose $500 each time, that's a loss of $10,000 over ten years. Would a $10,000 reward be enough for you to learn how to win? So, learn and pay yourself at least half of what you have previously been losing; $5,000 is still pretty good!

> *"You will become as small as your controlling desire; as great as your dominant aspiration."*
> *James Allen*

The first phase of your education in POWER BACCARAT 2 is complete. Now it is time to proceed to the next phase, practicing the application of the methods and techniques. Follow the 75-day practice plan in Chapter 22 as a blueprint. It will be time well spent if you are really serious about winning the next time you play.

When you have completed the practice plan, you will have a very good base of knowledge to build upon with each new play experience. You will also be quite a bit better than the average Baccarat player. You are now in the top 40! But, regular study and practice is a must if you want to continue to improve.

Finally, plan a trip, kick-butt, and have fun doing it. The effort put forth in getting to this point should pay-off well. Now Hit'em & Run!